Easy Homemade Desserts

*with Jell-O® brand pudding and pie filling
and Jell-O® brand instant pudding and pie filling*

Homemade Dessert The Easy Way

Wouldn't you like to pamper your family with homemade desserts every night? Those great homemade cakes they look forward to...those lavish parfaits and froze treats they love...their favorite pies? Lovely idea, but you just don't have the time? That's what this book is all about— homemade desserts that take little time and trouble, and taste delicious. And pudding is the building block that starts them all, makes the making easy, the results spectacular. Each recipe has been carefully selected and tested for taste, flavor appeal and ease of preparation in the test kitchens of the General Foods Consumer Center.

• How long do they take?

So you can see at a glance about how long it will take to make a particular dessert, each recipe has an estimated preparation time noted above it. This time includes baking time or any cooling time that is required before the recipe can be finished. (Chilling or freezing time needed before serving is not included.)

• Which pudding to use?

There are two kinds of pudding used for most recipes—Jell-O pudding and pie filling, which requires cooking, or Jell-O instant pudding and pie filling, which needs no cooking. Both work beautifully, but each works in different ways, with different preparation directions. To avoid confusion between pudding types, we've put a symbol by each in the ingredient listing:

★ for Jell-O pudding, which requires cooking
☆ for Jell-O instant pudding, which requires no cooking

And, to see how best to use each type of pudding, follow these pudding pointers.

Pudding Pointers for Cooked Pudding ★ Jell-O® brand pudding and pie filling

• When you cook the pudding...

stir the mixture as it cooks and be sure it comes to a _full_ boil. It's best to use an aluminum or stainless steel pan which heats evenly, without hot spots.

• If cooking should be interrupted...

you can remove the pudding from the heat—for up to 15 minutes. Then resume cooking as directed.

• For a thicker pudding...

cook and stir the mixture to a _full bubbling boil._ The cooled pudding will be thicker, firmer.

• The microwave way...

may be more convenient and can be used for all but the lemon flavor. Combine pudding mix and milk in a 4-cup glass measuring cup or medium-size glass bowl and blend well. Place in microwave oven and heat 3 to 4 minutes. Stir with rubber scraper or wooden spoon and continue to heat 2 to 4 minutes longer, until mixture comes to a boil. Remove from oven and chill.

- *After it's cooked…*
  the pudding will be thin, but it will thicken as it cools. If you wish to avoid having a film form on top, place plastic wrap directly on surface of the hot mixture.
- *To cool quickly…*
  place the pan of hot pudding in a larger pan of ice water and stir frequently until mix is cooled. Don't use this method for pie filling, however; the set will not be firm enough.
- *To mold pudding…*
  cool the cooked pudding 5 minutes, stirring twice, then pour into a plain mold or individual custard cups that have been rinsed in cold water. Chill. To unmold, dip mold or cup in hot water.
- *If you're counting calories…*
  you can use skim milk or reconstituted nonfat dry milk instead of whole milk. Pudding will be less rich, but you will save up to 35 calories per serving.
- *For extra creamy pudding…*
  beat the chilled pudding with a rotary beater before serving.
- *For extra rich pudding…*
  use light cream or half and half instead of whole milk.

Instant Pudding Pointers for ☆ Jell-O® brand instant pudding and pie filling
- *Start with cold milk…*
  it makes for a better consistency in the finished pudding. Beat slowly, not vigorously, then pour pudding into serving dishes or pie crust immediately after beating, unless the recipe calls for setting and then beating.
- *Even quicker…*
  is the blender method: put milk and pudding mix into container and blend at high speed for 15 seconds.
  Or the shaker method: use a 1-quart leakproof container, cover tightly and shake vigorously for at least 30 seconds.
- *Or use a fork…*
  just put mix into a 1-quart bowl and gradually add milk while stirring with a fork. Stir for 2 minutes.
- *If you're counting calories…*
  you can use cold skim milk or reconstituted nonfat dry milk instead of whole milk. The finished pudding will be somewhat leaner, but lower in calories.
- *For extra rich pudding…*
  use cold light cream or half and half instead of whole milk.

What's for dessert? If that's a question you hear a lot and are tired of answering with ho-hum replies, then this section is for you. For here are family desserts you can put together in minutes, without special shopping or planning, and come up with terrific results— quick parfaits, fruited puddings, frozen treats that can make any family meal a special one. Just turn to the kitchen cupboard for the secret. Start with pudding, the base that all these homemade desserts are built on. Then add ingredients from the cupboard— coconut, canned fruits, chopped nuts, cookies, graham crackers, candies, flavoring extracts, cereal— to give it your own flavor touch. Our two "Desserts with a Plus" sections (pages 6-7, for desserts that are cooked; pages 10-11 for desserts that need no cooking) give you some ideas, and you can come up with your own using family flavor favorites.

Or, turn to the refrigerator for further inspiration. Try cream cheese, sour cream, cottage cheese, whipped topping, yogurt, ice cream— and suddenly simple pudding puts on elegant airs. Use pudding, too, to whip up easy dessert sauces; they can turn a simple dish of fresh fruit into a memorable dessert, an ordinary pudding into a family treat.

You're a two-only family? Then finish your prepared pudding mix two ways, half with one flavor idea, half with another, so you have dessert for two meals. And if your family is on the large side, see our recipes, pages 12-14, designed to make a 4-serving package serve 6.

For starters, what could have more family appeal than a Peanut Butter and Jelly Pudding? Peanut butter flavors the pudding, and the pudding is marbled with the jelly— looks luscious and tastes even better.

PEANUT BUTTER AND JELLY DESSERT
🥛 *Less than 15 minutes to prepare*

2 cups cold milk
¼ cup creamy peanut butter
1 package (4-serving) ☆ Jell-O
   instant pudding— vanilla flavor

½ teaspoon water
¼ to ⅓ cup raspberry jelly
   or preserves*

*Or use grape or strawberry jelly or preserves

- Gradually beat milk into peanut butter in small bowl of electric mixer. Add pudding mix and beat at lowest speed about 2 minutes.
- Stir water into jelly. Layer pudding mixture and jelly into 5 parfait glasses. Chill. Garnish with whipped topping and chopped peanuts, if desired. Makes 5 servings.

Desserts With A Plus

Want a great family dessert in a hurry? Start with this basic recipe for cooked pudding ★, then add your own extra ingredients. We've suggested flavor combinations that work well, but you can do your own flavor mixing.

⬛ *From 15 to 30 minutes to prepare*

1 package (4-serving)* ★ Jell-O pudding — any flavor but lemon
2 cups milk

*Or use 6-serving size and 3 cups milk. Increase amounts of ingredients added 1½ times.

Combine pudding mix and milk in saucepan. Cook over medium heat, stirring constantly until pudding comes to a <u>full</u> boil. Pudding thickens as it cools. For creamier pudding place plastic wrap on surface of pudding while cooling and stir before serving.

FRUIT PARFAIT Try vanilla or banana cream flavor. Layer chilled pudding into parfait glasses with sweetened fresh or frozen fruit. Makes 4 servings.

EASY PEAR HELENE Use chocolate or milk chocolate flavor. Spoon chilled pudding into sherbet glasses. Place a drained, canned pear half on each. Drizzle with chocolate syrup. Makes 4 servings.

COOKIE SURPRISE Try butterscotch flavor. Mix 6 gingersnaps (or other cookies), crumbled, 6 tbs. chopped nuts and 2 tbs. melted butter. Put 1 tbs. of mix in each dessert dish. Spoon chilled pudding over crumbs. Top with remaining crumb mix. Makes 6 servings.

PUDDING À LA MODE Use chocolate or chocolate fudge flavor. Chill pudding in glasses. Top each with a scoop of vanilla ice cream before serving. Makes 4 or 5 servings.

QUICK PEACH MELBA Use vanilla or coconut cream flavor. Place drained peach half, cut side up, in each dessert dish. Put 1 tbs. raspberry jam or jelly in centers. Spoon chilled pudding over peaches. Add jam garnish. Makes 5 or 6 servings.

CRUNCHY PUDDING Use vanilla or French vanilla flavor. Add 1/3 cup Grape-Nuts brand cereal and 1 to 2 tbs. sugar to milk and pudding mix before cooking. Stir in 1/4 tsp. almond extract after removing from heat, if desired. Chill. Makes 4 servings.

BANANA SUNDAE Use banana cream flavor. Beat chilled pudding until smooth and layer into glasses with diced bananas and fudge sundae sauce. Makes 4 servings.

TOFFEE COFFEE PUDDING Use butterscotch flavor. Add 2 tbs. instant coffee and 2 tbs. sugar to milk and pudding mix before cooking. Fold 1/3 cup chopped nuts into chilled beaten pudding. Makes 4 servings.

ORANGE-CHOCOLATE DESSERT Use chocolate or milk chocolate flavor. Add 6 tbs. orange marmalade to beaten chilled pudding. Top with whipped topping. Makes 4 servings.

HONEY-COCONUT CREAM Use coconut cream flavor. Substitute 1/4 cup honey for 1/4 cup of the milk and add 1/8 tsp. cinnamon. Makes 4 servings.

CHOCOLATE MINT PUDDING Use chocolate or milk chocolate flavor. Add 1/4 tsp. peppermint extract to pudding after removing from heat. Serve chilled, garnished with whipped topping. Makes 4 servings.

CANDIED FRUIT PARFAIT Use vanilla or French vanilla flavor. Layer chilled pudding into glasses with chopped candied fruit. Makes 4 servings.

CHOCOLATE SOUR CREAM PUDDING

Add richness and style to chocolate pudding— piquant and special

From 15 to 30 minutes to prepare

1 package (6-serving) ★ Jell-O
   pudding— chocolate flavor
¼ cup sugar

¼ teaspoon salt
1½ cups water
1 cup (½ pt.) sour cream

- Combine pudding mix, sugar, salt and water in saucepan. Blend well. Cook and stir over medium heat until mixture comes to a <u>full</u> boil. Remove from heat. Cool 5 minutes, stirring once or twice.
- Stir in sour cream, blending well. Pour into bowl or individual serving dishes. Chill. Garnish with nutmeg, if desired. Makes 5 servings.

CREAMY COFFEE PUDDING

From 15 to 30 minutes to prepare

1 package (4-serving) ★ Jell-O
   pudding— vanilla flavor
1 tablespoon Maxwell House
   instant coffee

1½ cups milk
1 cup thawed Cool Whip
   non-dairy whipped
   topping

- Combine pudding mix, instant coffee and milk in saucepan. Cook and stir over medium heat until mixture comes to a <u>full</u> boil. Pour into bowl. Cover surface with plastic wrap and chill thoroughly.
- Beat chilled pudding slowly with rotary beater or wire whip until smooth. Fold in whipped topping. Spoon into individual dishes. Garnish with grated chocolate or chopped nuts, if desired. Makes 4 servings.

BITTERSWEET CHOCOLATE PUDDING

Cola takes the place of milk, adds a pleasant bittersweet flavor to this easy dessert

From 15 to 30 minutes to prepare

1 package (4-serving) ★ Jell-O
   pudding— chocolate flavor

1 cup water
1 bottle (6 ½ fl. oz.) cola beverage

- Combine pudding mix, water and cola beverage in saucepan. Cook and stir over medium heat until mixture comes to a <u>full</u> boil. Remove from heat. Pour into individual dessert dishes. Chill. Serve plain or with whipped topping, if desired. Makes 4 servings.

FAVORITE FLAVOR ICE CREAM

Just mix and freeze...that's all!

Less than 15 minutes to prepare

1 cup cold milk*
1 cup cold heavy cream*
2 tablespoons sugar

1 package (4-serving) ☆ Jell-O
   instant pudding—
   any flavor

*Or use 2 cups cold milk

- Combine milk, cream, sugar and pudding mix in bowl. Beat slowly with rotary beater or at lowest speed of electric mixer just until blended, about 1 minute. Pour into shallow pan and freeze until firm, at least 4 hours or overnight. Let stand at room temperature 15 minutes before serving. Makes 4 servings.

PUDDING FREEZE

Pudding gives you a head start in making this smooth and easy frozen dessert

📷 *Over 30 minutes to prepare*

1 package (4-serving) ★ Jell-O
pudding — any flavor
except lemon
¼ cup sugar

2 cups milk
1 container (4 ½ oz.)
Cool Whip non-dairy
whipped topping

- *Combine pudding mix, sugar and milk in saucepan. Cook and stir over medium heat until mixture comes to a <u>full</u> boil. Remove from heat. Cover surface with plastic wrap and chill.*
- *Beat chilled pudding until creamy and blend in whipped topping. Pour into 8x4-inch loaf pan. Freeze 1 hour.*
- *Spoon pudding into bowl and beat with rotary beater or electric mixer until smooth but not melted. Return to pan or put into 1-quart mold and freeze until firm, about 3 to 4 hours. Serve with ice cream sauce (p.46-47),if desired. Makes 6 to 8 servings.*

Instant Desserts With A Plus

Now make dessert magic with instant pudding ☆ — no cooking to it! Ingredients from your pantry shelf turn it into a family treat. Try our flavor suggestions, and make up your own.

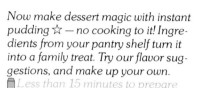 Less than 15 minutes to prepare

2 cups cold milk
1 package (4-serving)* ☆ Jell-O instant pudding

* Or use 6-serving size and 3 cups cold milk. Increase amounts of ingredients added 1½ times.

Combine milk and pudding mix in bowl. Beat slowly with rotary beater or at lowest speed of electric mixer until well blended, about 2 minutes. Chill in bowl or individual serving dishes. Pudding will be soft-set and ready to eat in 5 minutes. Store, covered, in refrigerator.

BUTTERSCOTCH CRUNCH Use butterscotch flavor. Fold ⅓ cup crushed peanut brittle into pudding before chilling. 4 servings.

ORANGE-WAFER DESSERT Try vanilla or coconut cream flavor. Crumble vanilla wafers (1 or 2 per dish) into dessert dishes. Fold in 1 can (11 oz.) mandarin orange sections, drained, or 1½ cups fresh orange sections, after beating pudding, saving 6 sections for garnish. Spoon pudding over wafers. Makes 6 servings.

BLACK-BOTTOM CRUNCH Try butter pecan flavor. Cut 5 chocolate-covered graham crackers into ½-inch squares and put in bottom of dessert dishes. Spoon beaten pudding over crackers. Makes 4 or 5 servings.

MARSHMALLOW-NUT PUDDING Use chocolate or chocolate fudge flavor. Let pudding set, then fold in 2 tbs. chopped nuts and ½ cup miniature marshmallows. Makes 5 servings.

LEMON EGGNOG PUDDING Use lemon flavor. Add ⅛ tsp. nutmeg and ½ tsp. rum extract to milk before beating with pudding. Makes 4 servings.

PRUNE PUDDING Use vanilla or French vanilla flavor. Fold in ½ cup slivered or chopped cooked prunes after preparing pudding. Makes 4 or 5 servings.

MINCEMEAT PARFAIT Use vanilla or French vanilla flavor. Layer pudding into parfait glasses with ½ cup moist mincemeat. Makes 5 servings.

TROPICAL PUDDING Try coconut cream flavor. Fold in ½ cup drained canned crushed pineapple after beating pudding. Garnish with flaked coconut. Makes 4 or 5 servings.

BANANA-WAFER DESSERT Use banana cream flavor. Layer pudding into dessert glasses with vanilla wafers and 1 banana, sliced. Top with whipped topping. Makes 4 servings.

PEPPERMINT PARFAIT Try vanilla or pineapple cream flavor. Let pudding set. Stir in 1 tbs. crushed peppermint candy. Layer pudding into parfait glasses with another 1 tbs. crushed peppermint candy. Makes 4 servings.

MOCHA PUDDING Use chocolate flavor. Add 1 to 2 tbs. instant coffee to milk before beating with pudding mix. Makes 4 servings.

COCONUT-FRUIT PUDDING Use vanilla or French vanilla flavor. Arrange drained canned apricot halves or peach slices in bottoms of dessert dishes. Fold ½ cup coconut into pudding after beating. Spoon over fruit. Makes 5 servings.

PISTACHIO-COCONUT PUDDING Use pistachio flavor. Fold in ½ cup toasted coconut after beating pudding. Garnish with additional toasted coconut. Makes 5 servings.

WANT TO SERVE SIX? ADD SOMETHING EXTRA

Serve six people from a four-serving package? It's easy. Just add ice cream,
or cream cheese, or whipped topping, or gelatin, or...what have you?

SUNDAE PUDDING

Ice cream is the plus here, makes a special, so easy, dessert

🥛 *Less than 15 minutes to prepare*

1 cup cold milk
1 package (4-serving) ☆ Jell-O
instant pudding — any flavor

1 pint ice cream — any flavor,
very soft

• *Combine milk and pudding mix in bowl. Beat slowly with rotary beater or at lowest*
speed of electric mixer until well blended, about 1 minute. Stir in ice cream. Chill
at least 15 minutes. Before serving, stir until creamy, if desired. Makes 6 servings.

FLAVOR COMBINATION SUGGESTIONS

Vanilla pudding with vanilla, coffee or pistachio ice cream
Butterscotch, butter pecan or banana cream pudding with vanilla or
butter pecan ice cream
Chocolate pudding with peppermint, vanilla or coffee ice cream
Coconut cream pudding with peach, vanilla or butter pecan ice cream
Lemon pudding with pistachio ice cream
Pistachio pudding with vanilla ice cream

PUDDING SWIRL

Add whipped topping for a marbled effect

🥛 *Less than 15 minutes to prepare*

1 package (4-serving) ☆ Jell-O
instant pudding —
any flavor*

2 cups cold milk
1 cup thawed Cool Whip
non-dairy whipped topping

* Or use ★ Jell-O pudding, any flavor except lemon

• *Prepare pudding mix with milk as directed on package. Let stand for 5 minutes.*
(If using cooked pudding, let chill.) Add whipped topping to pudding and stir
through for a marbled effect. Garnish with additional whipped topping, if desired.
Makes 6 servings.

PUDDING DELIGHT

Use whipped topping for a luscious layered look

🥛 *Less than 15 minutes to prepare*

1 package (4-serving) ☆ Jell-O
instant pudding —
any flavor*

2 cups cold milk
1 cup thawed Cool Whip
non-dairy whipped topping

* Or use ★ Jell-O pudding — any flavor except lemon

• *Prepare pudding mix with milk as directed on package. (If using cooked pudding,*
chill.) Pour half the pudding into 6 individual dessert dishes. Blend whipped
topping into remaining pudding and spoon into dishes. Chill. Garnish with
additional whipped topping, if desired. Makes 6 servings.

FAST AND FABULOUS FRUIT

Pudding, fruit and your choice of extras make this rich,
creamy and incredibly fast dessert

Less than 15 minutes to prepare

1 can (17 oz.) fruit cocktail
1 package (4-serving) ☆ Jell-O
instant pudding — lemon flavor

1 cup thawed Cool Whip
non-dairy whipped topping

• Reserve small amount of drained fruit for garnish, if desired. Combine pudding mix and rest of fruit cocktail, with syrup, in bowl. Blend in whipped topping. Garnish with reserved fruit. Makes 6 servings.

OTHER COMBINATION SUGGESTIONS

Start with any of the pudding flavors listed in the first column, add any fruit from the second column, with juice or syrup, and blend in any topping from the third column.

Coconut cream	1 can (20 oz.) crushed pineapple	1 cup sour cream
Lemon	in juice	1 cup whipped cream cheese
Vanilla	1 can (16 oz.) sliced peaches	1 cup cottage cheese
French vanilla	1 can (17 oz.) pitted dark	1 cup plain yogurt
	sweet cherries	1 cup prepared Dream Whip
	1 can (17 oz.) apricot halves, diced	whipped topping
		1 cup thawed Cool Whip
		non-dairy whipped topping

13

CREAMY CHEESE PUDDING

Try cream cheese for a quick mousse-like dessert

🧂 Less than 15 minutes to prepare

1 package (8 oz.) cream cheese, softened	**1 package (4-serving) ☆ Jell-O instant pudding— lemon,**
2 cups cold milk	**butter pecan, coconut cream, vanilla or pineapple cream flavor**

• Beat cream cheese until very soft. Gradually add ½ cup of the milk and blend until smooth. Add remaining milk and pudding mix. Beat slowly with rotary beater or at lowest speed of electric mixer until well blended, about 2 minutes. Pour immediately into individual dessert dishes and chill. Top each serving with a spoonful of jam, or sprinkle with nutmeg, if desired. Makes 6 servings.

FRUITY WHIP

Gelatin whipped till frothy gives pudding a party flavor

🧂 From 15 to 30 minutes to prepare

1 package (3 oz.) Jell-O brand gelatin— any flavor	**2 tablespoons lemon juice**
1 cup boiling water	**1 package (4-serving) ☆ Jell-O instant pudding— vanilla flavor**
½ cup cold water	**2 cups cold milk**

• Dissolve gelatin in boiling water. Add cold water and lemon juice.
• Combine pudding mix and milk in bowl. Beat slowly with rotary beater or at lowest speed of electric mixer until well blended, about 2 minutes.
• Set bowl of gelatin in larger bowl of ice and water. Stir until slightly thickened, then whip with rotary beater or electric mixer until fluffy and thick and double in volume. Blend pudding into whipped gelatin. Pour into serving bowl or individual dishes (do not mold). Chill until set. Makes 6 servings.

FRUITED TAPIOCA PUDDING

A refreshing plus for tapioca pudding...add canned fruit

🧂 Less than 15 minutes to prepare

1 can (8 ¾ oz.) fruit cocktail*	**1 package (3 ¼ oz.) Jell-O Americana**
1 can (8 ¼ oz.) crushed pineapple in syrup*	**vanilla tapioca pudding**
	1 tablespoon butter or margarine

* Or use 2 cups canned fruit— peaches, cherries or plums
• Drain fruits, reserving syrups. Add water to syrups to make 2 cups.
• Prepare pudding mix with measured liquid as directed on package. Remove from heat. Stir in butter and fruit. Chill. Makes 6 servings.

QUICK YOGURT AND PUDDING

🧂 Less than 15 minutes to prepare

1 cup cold milk	**1 package (4-serving) ☆ Jell-O**
1 container (8 oz.) yogurt	**instant pudding— any flavor**

• Combine milk and yogurt in bowl. Add pudding mix and beat slowly with rotary beater until blended, about 2 minutes. Pour into serving dishes and let stand for 5 minutes. Chill or serve at once. Makes about 4 servings.

APPLESAUCE PUDDING

This combines two family favorites, and it's ready in less than 10 minutes!

Less than 15 minutes to prepare

1½ cups cold milk
½ cup applesauce
Dash of salt
Dash of cinnamon

Dash of nutmeg
1 package (4-serving) ☆ Jell-O
   instant pudding—
   vanilla flavor

• Combine milk, applesauce, salt, cinnamon and nutmeg in bowl. Add pudding mix. Beat slowly with rotary beater or at lowest speed of electric mixer until well blended, about 2 minutes. Pour at once into serving dishes and let set about 5 minutes. Serve plain or garnish with graham cracker crumbs, if desired. Makes 4 servings.

LEMON CHEESE CUSTARD

Less than 15 minutes to prepare

1 package (3 oz.) Jell-O
   Americana golden egg
   custard mix
2 tablespoons sugar

1½ cups milk
1 package (8 oz.) cream
   cheese, cut in cubes
¾ teaspoon grated lemon rind

• Blend custard mix and sugar with milk in saucepan. Add cream cheese and lemon rind. Bring quickly to a boil, stirring constantly. Blend with rotary beater until smooth. Pour into custard cups. Chill until set. Serve with fresh sweetened berries, thawed frozen berries or canned pie filling, if desired. Makes 5 servings.

EASY SAUCES TO SPARK UP SIMPLE DESSERTS

Fruits or plain puddings or cakes become special family desserts with topping of quick-to-make sauces like these

---

BASIC CUSTARD SAUCE

Over 30 minutes to prepare

1 package (3 oz.) Jell-O Americana
   golden egg custard mix
1 tablespoon sugar

2¾ cups milk
1 egg, beaten
1 teaspoon vanilla

• Combine custard mix, sugar and milk in saucepan. Bring quickly to a boil, stirring constantly. Remove from heat. Stir small amount of the hot mixture into the beaten egg and mix well. Blend into remaining hot mixture. Place over low heat and cook and stir 1 minute longer. Add vanilla. Pour into bowl and cool about 30 minutes, stirring occasionally. Makes 3 cups.

CREAMY LEMON SAUCE

Less than 15 minutes to prepare

1 package (4-serving) ★ Jell-O
   pudding— vanilla flavor
3 cups milk

1 tablespoon sugar
½ teaspoon grated lemon rind
Dash of salt

• Combine all ingredients in saucepan. Cook and stir over medium heat until mixture comes to a boil. Cool, stirring often. Chill. Makes about 3 cups.

Better-Than-Ever Cakes

Pudding has revolutionized the whole world of cake baking, made cake from a mix taste better than ever. A few years ago home bakers discovered that adding instant pudding mix to cake mix gave cakes an extra richness and moistness, and a homemade taste that mix cakes never had before. Since then, that first cake with pudding added has been refined and made even better. Pudding and cake mix are the easy building blocks that have made such great results possible. In fact, cakes have never been so delicious, nor so easy.

On these pages you'll discover those very recipes that have changed home cake baking so. Start with the basic cake— using instant pudding mix to add moisture and a special flavor. Then add easy extras for flavor variations. "Cake With a Plus," pages 20-21, shows you how to go about it. But that's just the start. You'll find more recipes and ways to make cakes that are standouts— with pudding as a start, then sour cream, fruit, even vegetables from the garden, to add special flavor to the cake.

As for what goes on top of the cake, that's simple. Most pudding cakes are so moist and rich they need no more than a simple glaze or a dusting of confectioners sugar. For some, the "frosting" is baked right on the cake— couldn't be easier, or better. Sometimes it's poured on, or poked through the cake. Or, for special occasions, you might want a more spectacular topping, and pudding helps there, too, with very easy-to-make cake toppings. Or, use a cake sauce, as in this homemade Cranberry Loaf Cake with its own sauce topping.

CRANBERRY LOAF CAKE
Over 30 minutes to prepare

1 package (2-layer) yellow
    cake mix
1 package (4-serving) ☆ Jell-O
    instant pudding— lemon flavor
4 eggs
1 cup (½ pt.) sour cream
¼ cup oil
½ cup chopped nuts

1 can (16 oz.) whole berry
    cranberry sauce,
    broken into pieces
1 package (4-serving) ★ Jell-O
    pudding— lemon flavor
½ cup sugar
¼ teaspoon salt
1 tablespoon butter or margarine

• Combine cake mix, instant pudding mix ☆, eggs, sour cream, oil and nuts in large mixer bowl. Blend, then beat at medium speed of electric mixer for 4 minutes. Fold in half the cranberry sauce. Pour into two greased and floured 9x5-inch loaf pans. Bake at 350° for 50 to 55 minutes, or until cake tester inserted in center comes out clean and cake begins to pull away from sides of pan. Do not underbake. Cool in pans 15 minutes. Remove from pans and finish cooling on rack.

• Measure remaining cranberry sauce and add water to make 2½ cups. Combine pudding mix ★, sugar, salt and measured liquid in saucepan. Cook and stir over medium heat until mixture comes to a full boil and is thickened. Remove from heat. Stir in butter. Serve warm over cake slices. Makes 3 cups sauce.

HOMEMADE CAKE POINTERS

Want yours to be the best homemade cakes ever? Then follow the recipe directions carefully, beating just the time specified and baking at the correct temperature. If your cakes usually seem to take less or more time than the range specified for the particular pan used, you might want to have your oven's thermostat checked for accuracy. Other adjustments may have to be made for these special circumstances.

If you're using a pudding-included cake mix...

You probably will have to reduce the liquid ingredients. Reduce the water (or water substitute— such as orange juice or coffee) by ¼ cup. If sour cream is used rather than water, reduce that by ¼ cup. In some recipes no change is necessary and these recipes give the pudding-included cake mix as an alternate to the regular cake mix.

If you live in a high-altitude area...

You're probably used to making baking adjustments. Best results will come from experimentation, but for these cakes the usual ingredient adjustments are these: add all-purpose flour to the mix, ¼ to ⅔ cup (more for pudding-included mixes); add about ½ cup water (only ¼ cup if using pudding-included mix); reduce oil to about ¼ cup; and use large eggs. If sour cream is used, that amount should be reduced. And if any extra ingredients— such as raisins or nuts— are added, they should be finely chopped. Use the pan sizes recommended in the recipe and grease and flour pans well. In baking, raise the temperature about 25° for all but upside-down cakes, and test the cake carefully, as the baking time might be longer.

If you're using a different size pan...

rather than the pan called for in the recipe, the baking time will change. Use the cooking times given for the alternate cake pans in the "Cakes With a Plus" section, page 20, as a guide. Cakes baked in a smaller pan— 8-inch rather than 9-inch layers, for example— will take slightly longer, 5 to 10 minutes. For all cakes, the best test of doneness is that the cake has begun to pull away from sides of pan and a cake tester inserted in the center comes out clean, or cake springs back when lightly touched.

HOMEMADE TOPPINGS FOR YOUR CAKE

Luscious finishing touches and you can make them from pudding mix and ingredients on hand. See more glazes, fillings on pages 25, 72, 80, 82.

QUICK FLUFFY FROSTING

☐ *Less than 15 minutes to prepare*

1½ cups cold milk	**1 package (4-serving) ☆ Jell-O**
1 envelope Dream Whip	**instant pudding—**
whipped topping mix	**any flavor**

• Pour milk into deep narrow-bottom mixer bowl. Add whipped topping mix and pudding mix. Beat at low speed of electric mixer until well blended. Gradually increase beating speed to high and whip until mixture will form soft peaks, 4 to 6 minutes. Makes about 3 cups or enough to frost tops and sides of two 7-, 8- or 9-inch layers or a 13x9-inch cake. Store frosted cake in refrigerator.

CREAMY TOPPING

🔲 Less than 15 minutes to prepare

1 cup cold light cream or half and half
1¼ cups cold milk

1 package (4-serving) ☆ Jell-O instant pudding— any flavor

• *Pour cream and milk into bowl. Add pudding mix. Beat slowly with rotary beater or at lowest speed of electric mixer until blended, about 2 minutes. Let stand to set, about 5 minutes. Store in refrigerator in covered container. Just before serving, stir until creamy. Serve on cake, puddings or fruit. Makes about 2½ cups.*

QUICK-FIXING CHOCOLATE CAKE

🔲 Over 30 minutes to prepare

1 package (2-layer) chocolate cake mix or pudding-included cake mix
1 package (4-serving) ☆ Jell-O instant pudding— chocolate flavor
4 eggs

1¼ cups water
1 cup Baker's chocolate flavor baking chips
¼ cup oil
½ cup chopped nuts

• *Combine all ingredients in 13x9-inch pan and stir with fork until blended, at least 2 minutes. Bake at 350° for 40 to 45 minutes, or until cake springs back when lightly touched. Cool in pan, sprinkle with confectioners sugar, if desired.*

Cakes With A Plus

Here's the basic recipe that made cakes better than ever. Start with it, vary the pudding and cake mix flavors, then add easy extras for great results.

📖 *Over 30 minutes to prepare*

1 package (2-layer) cake mix
**1 package (4-serving) ☆ Jell-O
    instant pudding**
4 eggs
1 cup water
¼ cup oil

(For adjustments needed when using pudding-included cake mix or in high altitude areas, see page 18.)

Combine all ingredients in large mixer bowl. Blend, then beat at medium speed of electric mixer for 4 minutes. Pour into greased and floured 13x9-inch pan.* Bake at 350° for 40 to 45 minutes, or until cake springs back when lightly touched. Cool in pan about 15 minutes. Remove from pan and finish cooling on rack.

*Alternate baking pans:
    Two 9-inch layers for 30 to 45
    minutes; 10-inch tube or fluted
    tube pan for 50 to 55 minutes.

DOUBLE PISTACHIO CAKE Use pistachio pudding, white cake mix. Substitute 1 cup club soda for water and add ½ cup chopped nuts. Add Quick Fluffy Frosting (p. 18).

ORANGE CAKE Use vanilla pudding, yellow cake mix and 10-inch tube pan. Substitute ½ cup orange juice for 1 cup water and add 1 tbs. grated orange rind.

PUMPKIN CAKE Use butterscotch pudding, yellow cake mix. Reduce water to ¼ cup and add 1 cup canned pumpkin and 2 tsp. pumpkin pie spice. Serve with Creamy Topping (p. 18) and sprinkle with nutmeg.

CHOCOLATE CHIP CAKE Use chocolate pudding and chocolate cake mix. Stir 1 package (12 oz.) chocolate chips into batter. Sprinkle confectioners sugar on top.

TRIPLE LEMON CAKE Use lemon pudding, lemon cake mix, 10-inch tube pan. Add 1 tsp. lemon extract. Top with Tart Lemon Glaze (p. 72).

MOCHA CAKE Use chocolate pudding, yellow cake mix and 10-inch tube pan. Add 1 tbs. instant coffee to water before adding.

BUTTER PECAN CAKE Use butter pecan pudding and yellow cake mix. Add ½ tsp. imitation maple flavor to ingredients. Top with Quick Fluffy Frosting (p. 18), if desired.

PEANUT BUTTER CAKE Use vanilla pudding and yellow cake mix. Add 1 cup crunchy peanut butter to ingredients. Top with jelly or marmalade glaze.

SPICE SWIRL CAKE Use vanilla pudding and yellow cake mix and reduce water to ¾ cup. Mix ¼ cup packed brown sugar, ¾ tsp. cinnamon and ¼ tsp. nutmeg. Pour ⅔ of batter into 10-inch tube pan, sprinkle with sugar mix, then add remaining batter. Zigzag spatula through batter to marble.

COCONUT CAKE Use coconut cream or vanilla pudding, yellow cake mix and 10-inch tube or 13x9-inch pan. Stir 1 cup coconut into batter. Brush 1 tbs. heated honey on cooled cake. Sprinkle with ⅓ cup coconut.

NO FROSTING NEEDED...IT'S PART OF THE CAKE

No need to make a separate frosting with these cakes. The frosting's built
right in— baked on or poured on to make your cake-baking a snap.

TRIPLE CHOCOLATE-MARSHMALLOW CAKE

*Chocolatey, gooey...some call it "Mississippi Mud." Marshmallows bake on the top,
then get a second chocolate topping...mmm!*

■ *Over 30 minutes to prepare*

**1 package (2-layer) chocolate
   cake mix
1 package (4-serving) ☆ Jell-O
   instant pudding—
   chocolate flavor
1¾ cups milk
2 eggs**

**1 package (12 oz.) Baker's
   chocolate flavor
   baking chips
1 cup chocolate syrup
3 cups miniature
   marshmallows**

• Combine cake mix, pudding mix, milk, eggs and chips in large bowl. Mix by hand
until blended, about 2 minutes. Pour into greased and floured 13x9-inch pan.
Bake at 350° for 50 to 55 minutes, or until cake springs back when lightly touched.
Drizzle ½ cup of the chocolate syrup over the warm cake. Sprinkle marshmallows
evenly over syrup and bake 5 minutes longer or until marshmallows are softened
and lightly browned. Drizzle remaining syrup over marshmallows. Cool cake in pan
and cut into squares, using knife dipped in warm water.

CAKE-AND-SAUCE BAKE

This cake comes with its own sauce...and it's so easy to make

■ *Over 30 minutes to prepare*

**1 package (2-layer) yellow or
   devil's food cake mix or
   pudding-included cake mix
2 cups water
1½ cups milk**

**1 package (6-serving) ☆ Jell-O
   instant pudding—
   chocolate flavor
⅓ cup sugar
¼ to ½ teaspoon cinnamon**

• Prepare cake mix as directed on package. Pour batter into greased 13x9-inch pan.
Set aside.
• Pour water and milk into mixing bowl. Add pudding mix, sugar and cinnamon.
Beat slowly with rotary beater until well blended, 1 to 2 minutes. Pour over cake
batter. Bake at 350° for 1 hour or until cake tester inserted in center of cake comes
out clean. Cut into squares or spoon onto serving dishes while still warm.
Makes 12 servings.

PISTACHIO-MINT CAKE

Bright idea! Chocolate-covered mints melted on top make a delectable frosting

Over 30 minutes to prepare

1 package (2-layer) yellow
   cake mix
1 package (4-serving) ☆ Jell-O
   instant pudding—
   pistachio flavor
4 eggs
1 cup water
¼ cup oil

½ teaspoon peppermint
   extract
8 drops green food coloring
1 cup Baker's chocolate
   flavor baking chips,
   coarsely chopped
20 to 24 chocolate-covered
   thin mints

• *Combine cake mix, pudding mix, eggs, water, oil, extract and food coloring in large mixer bowl. Blend, then beat at medium speed of electric mixer for 4 minutes. Stir in chips. Pour into greased and floured 13x9-inch pan. Bake at 350° for 40 to 45 minutes, or until cake tester inserted in center comes out clean and cake begins to pull away from sides of pan. Do not underbake.*
• *Remove cake from oven and place candies in a single layer on top of cake to cover completely. Return to oven and bake 3 minutes longer to melt candies. Remove from oven and quickly spread melted candies evenly over cake. Cool, then cut into squares.*

RAINBOW CAKE

Moist white sheet cake with pretty and flavorful streaks of color

📷 Over 30 minutes to prepare

1 package (2-layer) white
   cake mix
1 package (4-serving) ☆ Jell-O
   instant pudding — vanilla flavor
4 eggs
1 cup water
¼ cup oil

1 package (3 oz.) Jell-O brand
   gelatin — any flavor
1 cup boiling water
1 cup cold water
1 container (4 ½ oz.) Cool Whip
   non-dairy whipped topping,
   thawed

• Combine cake mix, pudding mix, eggs, 1 cup water and oil in large mixer bowl. Blend, then beat at medium speed of electric mixer for 4 minutes. Pour into greased and floured 13x9-inch pan. Bake at 350° for 45 to 50 minutes, or until cake tester inserted in center comes out clean and cake begins to pull away from sides of pan. <u>Do not underbake.</u> Cool in pan about 15 minutes.
• Meanwhile, dissolve gelatin in boiling water. Add cold water. Poke holes in warm cake with utility fork at ½-inch intervals. Carefully pour gelatin over cake. Chill 3 to 4 hours. Spread whipped topping over top of cake.

LEMON SOUR CREAM POUND CAKE

📷 Over 30 minutes to prepare

1 package (2-layer) yellow cake mix
   or pudding-included cake mix
1 package (4-serving) ★ Jell-O
   pudding — lemon flavor

1 cup (½ pt.) sour cream
⅓ cup oil
4 eggs
Tart lemon glaze (p. 72)

• Combine cake mix, pudding mix, sour cream, oil and eggs in large mixer bowl. Blend at low speed of electric mixer just to moisten, scraping sides of bowl often. Then beat 3 minutes at medium speed. Pour batter into 10-inch tube pan which has been lined on bottom with paper. Bake at 350° for 55 minutes or until cake springs back when lightly touched. Cool in pan 15 minutes. Remove from pan and finish cooling on rack.
• Poke cake surface with cake tester and pour Tart Lemon Glaze over warm cake.

PINEAPPLE SOUR CREAM CAKE

📷 Over 30 minutes to prepare

1 can (8 oz.) crushed
   pineapple in juice
½ teaspoon baking soda
1 package (2-layer)
   yellow cake mix

1 package (4-serving) ☆ Jell-O
   instant pudding — pineapple
   cream, pistachio or vanilla flavor
4 eggs
1 cup (½ pt.) sour cream
¼ cup oil

• Combine pineapple with juice and soda, mixing well. Combine cake mix and remaining ingredients in large mixer bowl. Add pineapple mixture. Blend, then beat at medium speed of electric mixer for 4 minutes. Pour into greased and floured 10-inch fluted tube or tube pan. Bake at 350° for 50 to 55 minutes or until cake tester inserted in center comes out clean and cake begins to pull away from sides of pan. <u>Do not underbake.</u> Cool in pan 15 minutes. Remove from pan and finish cooling on rack.

BANANA BUTTER-PECAN CAKE

A winning combination of flavors makes this cake a favorite everywhere

🔲 *Over 30 minutes to prepare*

½ cup mashed banana
1 package (2-layer) yellow cake mix
1 package (4-serving) ☆ Jell-O
    instant pudding—
    butter pecan flavor

4 eggs
1 cup water
¼ cup oil
½ cup finely chopped
    nuts

• Combine all ingredients in large mixer bowl. Blend, then beat at medium speed of electric mixer for 4 minutes. Pour into greased and floured 10-inch fluted tube or tube pan. Bake at 350° for 50 minutes or until cake tester inserted in center comes out clean and cake begins to pull away from sides of pan. <u>Do not underbake.</u> Cool in pan 15 minutes. Remove from pan and finish cooling on rack. Sprinkle with confectioners sugar or top with Confectioners Sugar Glaze and garnish with banana slices and pecan halves, if desired.

CONFECTIONERS SUGAR GLAZE: Place 1 cup sifted confectioners sugar in small bowl. Add about 1 tablespoon hot milk gradually, blending well. Spread over top of cake and allow to run down sides. Makes ⅓ cup glaze or enough for a 9- or 10-inch tube or fluted tube cake, 8-inch square cake or two small pound cakes.

CHOCOLATE MAYONNAISE CAKE

An old favorite, made easy. Pudding, eggs and mayonnaise make it extra rich

🔲 *Over 30 minutes to prepare*

1 package (2-layer) devil's food
    cake mix
1 package (4-serving) ☆ Jell-O
    instant pudding — chocolate flavor

4 eggs
1 cup mayonnaise
1 cup water
1 cup chopped nuts

• Combine all ingredients in large mixer bowl. Blend, then beat at medium speed for 4 minutes. Pour into greased and floured 10-inch fluted tube or tube pan. Bake at 350° for 50 minutes, or until cake tester inserted in center comes out clean and cake begins to pull away from sides of pan. <u>Do not underbake.</u> Cool in pan 15 minutes. Remove from pan and finish cooling on rack.

PISTACHIO RIPPLE CAKE

🔲 *Over 30 minutes to prepare*

1 package (4-serving) ☆ Jell-O
    instant pudding—
    pistachio flavor
1 package (2-layer) yellow
    cake mix

4 eggs
1 cup (½ pt.) sour cream
¼ cup oil
½ cup raspberry or strawberry
    preserves

• Combine pudding mix, cake mix, eggs, sour cream and oil in large mixer bowl. Blend, then beat at medium speed of electric mixer for 4 minutes. Blend preserves into 1 cup of the batter. Pour half the pistachio batter into greased and floured 10-inch fluted tube pan. Spoon preserves batter into pan, away from sides of pan. Spoon on remaining pistachio batter. Zigzag a spatula through batter to marble. Bake at 350° for 50 minutes, or until cake tester inserted in center comes out clean and cake begins to pull away from sides of pan. <u>Do not underbake.</u> Cool in pan 15 minutes. Remove from pan and finish cooling on rack.

CARROT-PINEAPPLE CAKE

Moist, outrageously delicious...the pudding, carrots and pineapple do it

🥛 *Over 30 minutes to prepare*

1 package (2-layer) yellow
   cake mix
1 package (4-serving) ☆ Jell-O
   instant pudding— vanilla flavor
4 eggs
¼ cup oil

3 cups grated carrots
1 can (8 oz.) crushed pineapple
   in juice, drained
½ cup chopped nuts (optional)
1 teaspoon cinnamon
½ teaspoon salt

• *Combine all ingredients in large mixer bowl. Blend, then beat at medium speed of electric mixer for 4 minutes. Pour into greased and floured 10-inch fluted tube pan. Bake at 350° for 50 to 55 minutes or until cake tester inserted in center comes out clean and cake begins to pull away from sides of pan.* <u>Do not underbake.</u> *Cool in pan 15 minutes. Remove from pan and finish cooling on rack. Sprinkle with confectioners sugar, if desired.*

ZUCCHINI CAKE

A new favorite, with pudding and zucchini adding moistness and rich texture

🔲 *Over 30 minutes to prepare*

1 package (2-layer) yellow
   cake mix
1 package (4-serving) ☆ Jell-O
   instant pudding— vanilla flavor
4 eggs

¼ cup oil
3 cups grated zucchini
½ teaspoon salt
1½ teaspoons cinnamon
1 cup chopped nuts

• Combine all ingredients in mixer bowl. Blend, then beat at medium speed of electric mixer for 4 minutes. Pour into greased and floured 10-inch fluted tube or tube pan. Bake at 350° for 50 to 55 minutes, or until cake tester inserted in center comes out clean and cake begins to pull away from sides of pan. <u>Do not underbake.</u> Cool in pan 15 minutes. Remove from pan and finish cooling on rack. Sprinkle with confectioners sugar, if desired.

BANANA LOAF CAKES

A pair of moist loaf cakes…have one now, freeze one for later

🔲 *Over 30 minutes to prepare*

½ cup mashed banana
1 package (2-layer) yellow cake mix
1 package (4-serving) ☆ Jell-O
   instant pudding— banana
   cream or vanilla flavor

4 eggs
1 cup water
¼ cup oil
½ cup finely chopped nuts
   (optional)

• Combine all ingredients in large mixer bowl. Blend, then beat at medium speed of electric mixer for 4 minutes. Pour into two greased and floured 8x4-inch loaf pans. Bake at 350° for 50 to 55 minutes or until cake tester inserted in centers comes out clean and cake begins to pull away from sides of pans. <u>Do not underbake.</u> Cool in pans 15 minutes. Remove from pans and finish cooling on rack.

FRUITED COCONUT CAKE

🔲 *Over 30 minutes to prepare*

1 package (2-layer) yellow
   cake mix
1 package (4-serving) ☆ Jell-O
   instant pudding— lemon or
   vanilla flavor
1 can (16 oz.) fruit cocktail
2⅓ cups Baker's Angel Flake
   coconut

4 eggs
¼ cup oil
½ cup firmly packed brown
   sugar
½ cup chopped nuts (optional)
½ cup butter or margarine
½ cup granulated sugar
½ cup evaporated milk

• Combine cake mix, pudding mix, fruit cocktail with syrup, 1 cup of the coconut, eggs and oil in large mixer bowl. Blend, then beat at medium speed of electric mixer for 4 minutes. Pour into greased and floured 13x9-inch pan. Sprinkle with brown sugar and nuts. Bake at 325° for 45 minutes, or until cake tester inserted in center comes out clean and cake begins to pull away from sides of pan. <u>Do not underbake.</u> Cool in pan 15 minutes.
• Combine butter, granulated sugar and milk in saucepan. Bring to a boil and boil 2 minutes. Remove from heat. Stir in remaining coconut. Spoon warm sauce over warm cake. Serve warm or cool, with whipped topping, if desired.

Spectacular Pies

Melt-in-your-mouth cream pies, velvety rich ice cream pies, delectable cheese pies, luscious fruit pies— pudding is the building block that makes them all possible, and makes them so easy. Almost effortlessly, you can turn out pies your family will boast about, pies that turn an ordinary dinner into an occasion, pies that will be the highlight of your company dinners. Start with any crust— pastry, crumb or coconut— ready-made, from a package mix or your own (see recipes here and on the next page). Then the rest is simple. Try pudding with whipped topping or ice cream, for the creamiest pies ever. Or pudding with cream cheese or yogurt, for pies with a piquant plus. Or pudding with fruit— fresh, canned or frozen. The recipes are all here, and all so easy.

Don't like to bother with pie crust? Then meet the new Easier Pie (pages 39-41, 90-91), where the crust is an easy part of the pie. The crust might be crumbs, might be whole crackers or cookies, or the crust mix might be baked right with the pie. The whole idea is— less work for you, but with beautiful and delicious results.

Here's one of the quickest— and most popular— of pies, chocolate pie in a crunchy coconut crust.

CHOCOLATE-COCONUT PIE

🗎 Less than 15 minutes to prepare

1 package (6-serving) ☆ Jell-O
instant pudding—
chocolate flavor
2 ⅔ cups cold milk

1 baked 9-inch quick coconut
crust (recipe below)
1 cup thawed Cool Whip non-
dairy whipped topping

• Combine pudding mix and milk in bowl. Beat slowly with rotary beater or at lowest speed of electric mixer for 1 minute. Pour immediately into crust. Chill 1 hour. Garnish with whipped topping and chocolate curls, if desired.

QUICK COCONUT CRUST: Combine ¼ cup melted butter or margarine and 2 cups Baker's Angel Flake coconut. Press evenly into ungreased 8-or 9-inch pie pan. Bake at 350° for 20 to 30 minutes, or until golden brown. Cool. For ease in serving, dip pie pan in warm water for a few seconds before cutting.

EASY PIE POINTERS

Spectacular pies are no problem to make this easy pudding way. Just follow these directions carefully. Remember to refrigerate any leftover pie.

• If using cooked pudding mix...

For an 8-inch pie shell, use the 4-serving size pudding mix; for a 9-inch shell, use the 6-serving size and reduce milk to 2¾ cups. Cook and stir the pudding mix and milk mixture to a <u>full bubbling boil</u>. Let stand 5 minutes, stirring twice, then pour into the baked cooled shell and chill 3 hours. The lemon flavor mix has different directions that call for eggs, sugar and water rather than milk. Follow package directions to make a basic lemon meringue pie. For an extra-special version, see page 58.

• If using instant pudding mix...

For an 8-inch pie shell, use the 4-serving size pudding mix (decrease the amount of milk to 1¾ cups for chocolate, chocolate fudge and butterscotch flavors). For a 9-inch shell, use the 6-serving size mix (decrease milk to 2⅔ cups for all flavors excep vanilla, lemon and butter pecan). Beat only 1 minute to blend, then pour into the baked and cooled pie shell right away. Chill 1 hour.

• Have the wrong size pie pan?

If your pie shell is smaller than that called for in the recipe, you can pour the excess filling into an individual tart shell or custard cup (lined with crumb mix, if you wish). If your shell is larger than that called for, you might add whipped topping to the chilled pie before serving. Or double the recipe and use excess for individual cups.

• As for the pie crust...

Our tested foolproof recipe follows. See, too, Quick Coconut Crust and Crumb Crust pages 29, 31. Don't like to make pie crust? You can buy excellent ready-made ones.

PIE SHELL

Over 30 minutes to prepare

1¼ cups unsifted all-purpose flour	½ cup shortening
½ teaspoon salt	3 tablespoons (about) cold water

• Measure flour and salt into bowl. Lightly cut in shortening with pastry blender until mixture resembles coarse meal. Sprinkle in water, a small amount at a time, mixing lightly with pastry blender or fork until all particles are moistened and cling together when pastry is pressed into a ball. Cover with damp cloth and let stand a few minutes, or chill.

• Roll pastry on lightly floured board into a thin circle (less than ⅛-inch thick). Line 8-, 9- or 10-inch pie pan. Trim pastry 1 inch larger than pan and fold under to form a standing rim. Flute edge.

FOOD PROCESSOR METHOD: Use steel blade of processor. Place flour, salt and shortening in processor bowl and blend, turning machine on and off, until mixture has consistency of coarse meal. With motor on, add cold water gradually until dough forms a ball. Then proceed as directed above.

BAKED PIE SHELL: Prick pastry very thoroughly on bottom, sides and in bottom curve, using a fork. To prevent shrinkage of pastry, place a second pie pan directly over pastry, or line pastry shell with brown paper or double layer of cheese cloth and partially fill with rice or dried beans. Bake at 450° for 15 minutes. Remove lining or pie pan and bake 5 minutes longer or until lightly browned. Cool before filling.

TART SHELLS: Cut rolled pastry into 5- or 6-inch circles. Carefully fit on outside of inverted tart or muffin pans. Trim edges. Prick thoroughly with a fork. Place pans on baking sheet and bake at 450° for 12 to 15 minutes, or until pastry is lightly browned. Makes 4 or 5.

CREAMY APRICOT PIE

🕐 *Over 30 minutes to prepare*

1 can (16 oz.) apricot halves
1 package (4-serving) ★ Jell-O
   pudding — vanilla flavor
1 package (3 oz.) Jell-O brand
   gelatin — apricot flavor

1 envelope Dream Whip whipped
   topping mix
1 baked 9-inch graham cracker
   crumb crust, cooled

- Drain apricots, reserving syrup. Add water to syrup to make 2 cups. Set aside 3 apricot halves for garnish and dice remaining apricots.
- Combine pudding mix, gelatin and measured liquid in medium saucepan. Cook and stir over medium heat until mixture comes to a full boil. Pour into bowl and chill well. (To hasten chilling time, place bowl in larger bowl of ice and water and stir until thickened.)
- Meanwhile, prepare whipped topping mix as directed on package. Fold into chilled pudding mixture. Fold in diced apricots. Spoon into crust and chill about 2 hours. Garnish with apricots and topping, if desired.

CRUMB CRUST: Combine 1 cup fine graham cracker, chocolate wafer or ginger-snap crumbs and 3 tablespoons sugar. Mix in 3 to 4 tablespoons softened butter or margarine. Press firmly on bottom and sides of 8-inch pie pan. (For 9- or 10-inch pan, increase crumbs to 1¼ cups and sugar and butter to ¼ cup each.) For unbaked crust, chill 1 hour before filling. For baked crust, bake at 375° for 8 minutes; cool thoroughly before filling. To ease serving, dip pan in warm water before cutting.

STRAWBERRY CREAM PIE

A spectacular way with fresh strawberries, and you make it in minutes

▇ Less than 15 minutes to prepare

1 pint strawberries, hulled
1 package (4-serving) ☆ Jell-O
   instant pudding—
   coconut cream, vanilla or
   French vanilla flavor
1½ cups cold milk

1 container (4½ oz.)
   Cool Whip
   non-dairy
   whipped topping
1 baked 9-inch pie shell,
   cooled

- Set aside 1 cup of the strawberries for garnish. Quarter or slice remaining berries.
- Combine pudding mix and milk in bowl. Beat slowly with rotary beater or at lowest speed of electric mixer for 1 minute. Blend in ½ cup of the whipped topping. Fold in quartered strawberries and pour into pie shell. Chill at least 3 hours. Top with remaining whipped topping and garnish with the whole strawberries.

BLUEBERRY CREAM PIE

Fresh blueberries top an easy cream pie

▇ Over 30 minutes to prepare

1 package (4-serving) ★ Jell-O
   pudding— vanilla flavor
2 cups milk
1 baked 9-inch pie shell, cooled
2 cups fresh or frozen
   blueberries

½ cup water
½ cup sugar
2 tablespoons cornstarch
   Dash of cinnamon
   Dash of salt
1 tablespoon lemon juice

- Combine pudding mix and milk in saucepan. Cook and stir over medium heat until mixture comes to a <u>full bubbling boil</u>. Remove from heat and cool 5 minutes, stirring twice. Pour into pie shell and cool.
- Meanwhile, combine blueberries and water in saucepan. Bring to a boil. Mix sugar with cornstarch, cinnamon and salt. Add to berries and continue cooking until mixture is clear and thickened, stirring constantly. Remove from heat and add lemon juice. Spoon at once over cooled filling. Chill. Garnish with prepared whipped topping and flaked coconut, if desired.

BERRY-TOPPED CREAM PIE

Simple to make with frozen or fresh fruit, but a very special dessert

▇ Less than 15 minutes to prepare

1 package (6-serving) ☆ Jell-O
   instant pudding—
   vanilla flavor*
3 cups cold milk

1 baked 9-inch graham cracker
   crumb crust, cooled
1 package (10 oz.) Birds Eye
   quick thaw strawberries or
   red raspberries, thawed**

*Or use ★ Jell-O pudding— vanilla flavor
** Or use sweetened fresh blueberries, strawberries, or sliced peaches

- Prepare pudding mix with milk as directed on package for pie. Pour into crust and chill. Just before serving cut into 6 to 8 wedges and top each with berries.

EASY FRUIT TARTS
Use fresh or canned fruit for this quick and elegant dessert

🔲 *Over 30 minutes to prepare*

1 package (4-serving) ☆ Jell-O
    instant pudding— vanilla or
    lemon flavor*
2 cups cold milk
8 baked 3-inch tart shells, cooled

1 to 2 cups fruit
1 package (3 oz.) Jell-O
    brand gelatin — strawberry,
    raspberry, orange or
    apricot flavor

Or use ★ Jell-O pudding— vanilla flavor

• Prepare pudding mix with milk as directed on package. (If using cooked pudding, chill.) Divide evenly among tart shells. Arrange fruit on pudding. Chill.
• Prepare gelatin as directed on package. Chill until thickened. Spoon over fruit on tarts to glaze. (Chill any remaining gelatin to use at another time.) Chill tarts until ready to serve. Garnish with whipped topping, if desired. Makes 8 tarts.

SUGGESTED FRUIT COMBINATIONS
Blueberries with grapes, peaches or whole strawberries
Whole strawberries alone or with grapes or bananas
Layered peach slices
Apricot halves and mint sprigs
Canned pineapple slice and stemmed bing cherry
Green grapes and mandarin orange sections

PINEAPPLE SOUR CREAM PIE

A uniquely rich flavor combination...and a cinch to make

Less than 15 minutes to prepare

1 package (6-serving) ☆ Jell-O
   instant pudding – vanilla flavor
1 can (8 oz.) crushed pineapple
   in juice

2 cups (1 pt.) sour cream
1 tablespoon sugar
1 baked 9-inch pie shell,
   cooled

• Combine pudding mix, pineapple with juice, sour cream and sugar in deep narrow bottom bowl. Beat slowly with rotary beater or at lowest speed of electric mixer for 1 minute. Pour into pie shell. Chill about 3 hours. Garnish with whipped topping, additional pineapple or maraschino cherries, if desired.

QUICK CHERRY PIE

An easy cherry pie...just cook the filling in minutes

From 15 to 30 minutes to prepare

1 package (6-serving) ★ Jell-O
   pudding – vanilla flavor
¼ cup sugar
¼ teaspoon salt
1 cup water
1 tablespoon lemon juice

1 can (16 oz.) pitted red sour
   cherries
1 tablespoon butter or margarine
Few drops red food coloring
   (optional)
1 baked 9-inch pie shell, cooled

• Combine pudding mix, sugar and salt in saucepan. Stir in water and lemon juice and blend well. Add cherries and cherry liquid. Cook and stir over medium heat until mixture comes to a <u>full</u> boil. Remove from heat. Stir in butter and food coloring. Cool 5 minutes. Pour into pie shell. Let stand at least 4 hours, or until set, or chill several hours. Garnish with whipped topping, if desired.

LEMON YOGURT PIE

Lemon meringue pie with the refreshing tang of yogurt

From 15 to 30 minutes to prepare

1 package (6-serving) ★ Jell-O
   pudding – lemon flavor
1 cup sugar
¼ cup water
3 egg yolks
2 cups water

1 container (8 oz.)
   plain yogurt
1 baked 9-or 10-inch
   pie shell, cooled
3 egg whites
6 tablespoons sugar

• Combine pudding mix, 1 cup sugar and ¼ cup water in saucepan. Blend in egg yolks, 2 cups water and yogurt, blending well. Cook and stir over medium heat until mixture comes to a <u>full bubbling boil.</u> Cool 5 minutes, stirring twice. Pour into pie shell.

• Beat egg whites until foamy throughout. Gradually beat in 6 tablespoons sugar and continue beating until mixture will form stiff shiny peaks. Spread over pie filling, sealing well at edges. Bake at 425° until meringue is delicately browned, about 5 minutes. Cool 4 hours before cutting.

CREAMY CHEESE PIE

It's like cheesecake in a pie shell

Less than 15 minutes to prepare

1 package (6-serving) ★ Jell-O
   pudding— chocolate or
   vanilla flavor
2 tablespoons sugar

2 ½ cups milk
1 package (8 oz.) cream cheese,
   softened
1 baked 9-inch pie shell, cooled

• Combine pudding mix, sugar and milk in saucepan. Cook and stir over medium heat until mixture comes to a *full bubbling boil*. Add hot pudding gradually to cream cheese, blending until smooth. Pour into pie shell. Chill at least 3 hours. Garnish with whipped topping, if desired.

QUICK CHEESE PIE

Even faster...with that rich cheesecake flavor

Less than 15 minutes to prepare

1 package (8 oz.) cream cheese, softened
2 cups cold milk
1 package (4-serving) ☆ Jell-O
   instant pudding— lemon, coconut
   cream or pineapple cream flavor

1 baked 9-inch graham
   cracker crumb crust
   or pie shell,
   cooled

• Beat cream cheese until very soft. Gradually add ½ cup of the milk and blend until smooth. Add remaining milk and pudding mix. Beat slowly with rotary beater or at lowest speed of electric mixer for 1 minute. Pour immediately into crust. Chill until firm, at least 2 hours. Sprinkle with nutmeg, if desired.

LEMON CHEESE PIE

Add lemon for a tangy twist to cheese pie

Less than 15 minutes to prepare

1 package (6-serving) ★ Jell-O
   pudding— lemon flavor
¾ cup sugar
1 egg, slightly beaten

3 cups water
1 package (8 oz.) cream cheese,
   softened
1 baked 10-inch pie shell, cooled

• Combine pudding mix and sugar in saucepan. Blend in egg and water. Cook and stir over medium heat until mixture comes to a *full bubbling boil*. Add hot mixture gradually to cream cheese, blending until smooth. Pour into pie shell. Cover with plastic wrap. Chill at least 3 hours. Garnish with whipped topping, if desired.

EGGNOG PIE

A festive holiday dessert you can make in minutes

Less than 15 minutes to prepare

1 ½ cups cold dairy or
   canned eggnog
1 ½ cups cold milk

1 package (6-serving) ☆ Jell-O
   instant pudding— vanilla flavor
1 baked 9-inch pie shell, cooled

• Pour eggnog and milk into bowl. Add pudding mix. Beat slowly with rotary beater or at lowest speed of electric mixer for 1 minute. Pour at once into pie shell. Chill at least 1 hour. Garnish with whipped topping and sprinkle with nutmeg, if desired.

ICE CREAM PUDDING PIE

Try several flavor combinations with this scrumptious pie

🮙 *Less than 15 minutes to prepare*

1½ cups cold milk	1 baked 9-inch
1 cup (½ pt.) ice cream—	pie shell or
any flavor, softened	graham cracker
1 package (6-serving)* ☆ Jell-O	crumb crust,
instant pudding— any flavor	cooled

° *Or use two 4-serving size packages, 2 cups milk, 1½ cups ice cream*

• *Thoroughly blend milk and ice cream in bowl. Add pudding mix. Beat slowly with rotary beater or at lowest speed of electric mixer until blended, about 1 minute. Pour immediately into pie shell. Chill until set, about 3 hours. Garnish with whipped topping, if desired.*

FLAVOR COMBINATION SUGGESTIONS

Vanilla pudding with coffee, vanilla, pistachio, cherry-vanilla or butter pecan ice cream
Chocolate pudding with vanilla, coffee, peppermint or chocolate ice cream
Banana cream pudding with butter pecan ice cream
Lemon pudding with pistachio ice cream
Butter pecan pudding with butter pecan or vanilla ice cream

FROZEN PISTACHIO MERINGUE PIE

Like Baked Alaska in a pie...the filled pie is frozen with meringue added just before serving

🕐 Over 30 minutes to prepare

1 package (4-serving) ☆ Jell-O
   instant pudding—
   pistachio flavor
2 cups cold milk

1 baked 8-inch pie shell, cooled
   or quick coconut crust (p. 29)
2 egg whites
2 tablespoons sugar

• Combine pudding mix and milk in bowl. Beat slowly with rotary beater or at lowest speed of electric mixer for 1 minute. Pour immediately into pie shell. Freeze at least 3 hours.

• Beat egg whites until foamy throughout. Gradually beat in sugar and continue beating until soft peaks form. Spread over pie filling, sealing well at edges. Bake at 400° for about 10 minutes. Serve at once.

MARSHMALLOW-NUT ICE CREAM PIE

Rich chocolate pie with a marshmallow-nut bottom, for kids of all ages

🕐 Less than 15 minutes to prepare

½ cup marshmallow topping
1 baked 9-inch pie shell,
   cooled
¼ cup chopped nuts
1½ cups cold milk

1 cup (½ pt.) chocolate ice cream,
   softened
1 package (6-serving) ☆ Jell-O
   instant pudding—
   chocolate flavor

• Spread marshmallow topping in bottom of pie shell, using knife dipped in warm water. Sprinkle with nuts.

• Blend milk and ice cream in bowl thoroughly. Add pudding mix. Beat slowly with rotary beater or at lowest speed of electric mixer until blended, about 1 minute. Pour immediately into pie shell. Chill until set, about 3 hours. Garnish with whipped topping, if desired.

DELUXE CREAM PIE

Gelatin adds a tangy fruit flavor to this creamy pie

🕐 Over 30 minutes to prepare

1 package (4-serving) ★ Jell-O
   pudding— vanilla, coconut
   cream or banana
   cream flavor
1 package (3 oz.) Jell-O brand
   gelatin— any flavor

2¼ cups water
1 container (4½ oz.) Cool Whip
   non-dairy whipped
   topping, thawed
1 baked 9-inch pie shell,
   cooled

• Combine pudding mix, gelatin and water in saucepan. Cook and stir over medium heat until mixture comes to a <u>full</u> boil and is thickened and clear. Remove from heat and chill until slightly thickened.

• Blend whipped topping thoroughly into chilled filling mixture. Spoon into pie shell. Chill until firm, at least 3 hours.

FLAVOR COMBINATION SUGGESTIONS
Vanilla pudding with strawberry or lime gelatin
Coconut cream pudding with orange-pineapple gelatin
Banana cream pudding with strawberry-banana gelatin

PIE DELIGHT

A beautiful creamy layered pie...no one would guess it's so easy to make

From 15 to 30 minutes to prepare

1 package (6-serving) ☆ Jell-O
instant pudding—
butter pecan, chocolate,
chocolate fudge or
vanilla flavor*
2½ cups cold milk

1 baked 9-inch pie shell
or graham cracker
crumb crust, cooled
1 cup thawed Cool Whip
non-dairy whipped
topping

*Or use ★ Jell-O pudding—banana cream, chocolate,
chocolate fudge or vanilla flavor

• Prepare pudding mix with 2½ cups milk as directed on package for pie. Measure 1 cup and set aside. (If using cooked pudding, cover with plastic wrap and chill thoroughly.) Pour remaining mixture into pie shell and chill.

• Blend whipped topping into the measured pie filling. Spread over chilled filling in pie shell. Chill about 3 hours. Garnish with additional whipped topping, if desired.

MARBLE CREAM PIE

Two flavors swirl together in this easily made pie

From 15 to 30 minutes to prepare

1 package (4-serving) ★ Jell-O
pudding—vanilla,
coconut cream,
banana cream or
butterscotch flavor*

1 package (4-serving) ★ Jell-O
pudding—chocolate or
chocolate fudge flavor*
3 cups milk
1 baked 9-inch pie shell, cooled

*Or use ☆ Jell-O instant pudding, same flavors

• Prepare vanilla and chocolate pudding mixes <u>separately</u> as directed on package for pie, using 1½ cups milk for each. Spoon at once into pie shell by tablespoonfuls, alternating the two flavors. Cut through fillings with knife or spatula in wide zigzag course. Repeat zigzag in opposite direction. Chill about 3 hours (or at least 1 hour for instant pudding). Garnish with whipped topping and chocolate curls, if desired.

COCONUT CRUNCH PIE

Cream pie with a difference...a crunchy coconut-praline topping

Over 30 minutes to prepare

1 package (6-serving) ★ Jell-O
pudding—vanilla flavor
2 ¾ cups milk
1 baked 9-inch pie shell,
cooled

1 cup Baker's Angel Flake
coconut
3 tablespoons brown sugar
1 ½ tablespoons butter or
margarine

• Combine pudding mix and milk in saucepan. Cook and stir over medium heat until mixture comes to a <u>full bubbling boil</u>. Remove from heat and cool 5 minutes, stirring twice. Pour into pie shell. Chill at least 4 hours.

• Combine coconut, brown sugar and butter in saucepan. Cook and stir until coconut is golden brown. Remove from heat and stir with fork for a few minutes to cool slightly. Sprinkle evenly over pie filling.

NOW...THE EASIER PIE

The pie that takes the crust-making work out of pie making. It might be square, might be round, but the results are delicious. Now homemade pie is "easier than pie."

LEMON CRUMB EASIER PIE

Graham cracker crumbs and nuts make the easier crust in this square pie

▨ *Over 30 minutes to prepare*

1 cup fine graham cracker crumbs
⅓ cup finely chopped pecans
2 tablespoons sugar
¼ cup butter or margarine, melted
1 package (4-serving) ★ Jell-O
    pudding — lemon flavor

½ cup sugar
¼ cup water
1 egg
2 cups water
1 tablespoon butter
    or margarine

- Combine crumbs, pecans and 2 tablespoons sugar. Add melted butter and blend well. Press two-thirds of mixture firmly on bottom of 8-inch square pan. Bake at 375° for 5 minutes. Cool.
- Combine pudding mix, ½ cup sugar and ¼ cup water in saucepan. Add egg and blend well. Add 2 cups water. Cook and stir over medium heat until mixture comes to a <u>full bubbling boil</u> and is thickened, about 5 minutes. Remove from heat. Add 1 tablespoon butter and blend well. Cool 5 minutes, stirring twice. Pour over baked crumb mixture. Sprinkle with remaining crumbs. Chill until firm. Cut into squares. Serve with whipped topping, if desired. Makes 9 servings.

EASIER PEACH PIE

No pie crust to roll! Just sprinkle the mix in the pan and it bakes with the filling!

▨ *Over 30 minutes to prepare*

1 cup pie crust mix
1 can (17 oz.) peach
    slices
¼ cup milk

1 package (4-serving) ★ Jell-O
    pudding — vanilla, coconut
    cream or butterscotch flavor
½ teaspoon ground allspice

- Sprinkle ½ cup of pie crust mix over bottom of 8-inch pie pan.
- Drain peaches, reserving syrup. Cut peaches into small pieces.
- Combine milk, pudding mix, reserved syrup and allspice, blending well. Stir in peaches. Spoon half the mixture over pie crust mix in pan. Sprinkle with remaining pie crust mix and top with remaining pudding mixture. Bake at 375° for 45 minutes or until set. Makes 6 to 8 servings.

CHERRY-TOPPED EASIER PIE

Whole graham crackers made the "crust" in this beautiful layered pie

📖 *From 15 to 30 minutes to prepare*

14 whole graham crackers
1 package (6-serving) ☆ Jell-O
   instant pudding—
   vanilla flavor

2 cups cold milk
1 cup thawed Cool Whip non-
   dairy whipped topping
1 can (21 oz.) cherry pie filling

- Line 9-inch square pan with whole graham crackers, breaking crackers if necessary, to fill pan.
- Combine pudding mix and milk in bowl. Beat slowly with rotary beater or at lowest speed of electric mixer until well blended, about 2 minutes. Let stand 5 minutes, then blend in whipped topping. Spread half the pudding mixture over crackers. Add another layer of crackers. Top with remaining pudding mixture and remaining crackers. Top with cherry pie filling. Chill 3 hours. Makes 9 servings.

STRAWBERRY LAYERED EASIER PIE

Cracker crust on the bottom, and in the middle, too

From 15 to 30 minutes to prepare

9 whole graham crackers
1 package (6-serving) ☆ Jell-O
  instant pudding—
  vanilla flavor
2 cups cold milk

1 container (4 ½ oz.) Cool Whip
  non-dairy whipped
  topping, thawed
1 cup finely chopped
  strawberries

- Arrange 9 cracker halves in bottom of 9-inch square pan.
- Combine pudding mix and milk in bowl. Beat slowly with rotary beater or at lowest speed of electric mixer until well blended, about 2 minutes. Fold in 1 cup of whipped topping. Pour half the pudding mixture over crackers in pan. Top with strawberries.
- Arrange remaining crackers on berries and add remaining pudding mixture. Spread remaining whipped topping over the top. Garnish with halved strawberries, if desired. Chill. Cut into squares. Makes 9 servings.

EASIER BROWNIE PIE

A crustless pie...extra rich and chocolatey

Over 30 minutes to prepare

⅓ cup butter or margarine
⅓ cup sugar
1 egg
1 square Baker's
  semi-sweet chocolate,
  melted and cooled

1 package (4-serving) ★ Jell-O
  pudding—chocolate
  fudge flavor
¼ cup all-purpose flour
¼ cup chopped nuts
½ teaspoon vanilla

- Cream butter. Gradually beat in sugar and continue beating until light and fluffy. Add egg and beat well. Blend in chocolate. Add pudding mix and flour, beating until smooth. Stir in nuts and vanilla. Pour into ungreased 8-inch pie pan. Bake at 325° for about 30 minutes or until edges begin to pull away from sides of pan. Cool and serve with ice cream or whipped topping, if desired. Makes 6 servings.

EASIER PUDDING TARTS

A new kind of tart you can whip up in a jiffy

From 15 to 30 minutes to prepare

½ cup cookie or cracker
  crumbs
2 to 3 teaspoons butter or
  margarine, melted

1 package (4-serving) ☆ Jell-O
  instant pudding—
  any flavor
2 cups cold milk

- Combine crumbs and butter. Press mixture on bottom and sides of individual dessert dishes.
- Combine pudding mix and milk in bowl. Beat slowly with rotary beater or at lowest speed of electric mixer until well blended, about 2 minutes. Spoon into crumb-lined dishes. Chill. Garnish with whipped topping and additional crumbs, if desired. Makes 4 servings.

FLAVOR COMBINATION SUGGESTIONS

Lemon, vanilla or chocolate pudding with graham cracker crumbs
Vanilla pudding with chocolate wafer, gingersnap or chocolate sugar cookie crumbs
Chocolate or vanilla pudding with vanilla wafer crumbs

Between-Time Treats

What to give the kids when they're just home from school and ravenous? What homemade extra to serve with the coffee when it's your turn for the club meeting? What "finger food" to make for the church social?

To the rescue, these versatile and delicious treats for all those between-meal occasions, all homemade and easy. For the kids, try one of the frozen treats— cones, pops or frozen sandwiches, simple to make ahead and have on hand. Or a terrific milk shake you can whip up in a jiffy. For those meetings— a super coffee cake, or crisp, flavorful cookies. Sound good? They are, and pudding is the building block that makes them possible...and easy. In these recipes, there's lots of goodness in exciting new forms to meet any occasion. Try them and see how they go over with your audience.

FROZEN PUDDING TREATS
Easy, good and wholesome, too...the perfect snack for kids

📖 Less than 15 minutes to prepare

**1 package (4-serving) ☆ Jell-O   2 cups cold milk or
instant pudding — any flavor   half and half**

• Combine pudding mix and milk in bowl. Beat slowly with rotary beater or at lowest speed of electric mixer until well blended, about 2 minutes. Pour into six 5-ounce paper cups. Insert wooden or plastic spoon into each for a handle. Press a square of aluminum foil or wax paper down onto pudding to cover, piercing center of foil with handle. Freeze until firm, at least 5 hours. Press firmly on bottom of cup to release pop. Serve with foil around handle. Makes 6 pops.

SPECIAL ADDITIONS
Before pouring mixture into cups, add any of these:
¼ cup chopped nuts, crushed peppermint candy or chocolate sprinkles
⅓ cup crushed peanut brittle
½ cup miniature marshmallows, chunky peanut butter or chopped or mashed fruit
Or marble into mixture ¼ cup jam or ⅓ cup sundae sauce
Or place 1 tablespoon chopped nuts in each cup before adding pudding
Or roll frozen pops in crushed peppermint candy or chocolate sprinkles

43

MARBLED ORANGE POPS

Add orange flavor to vanilla for these easy pops

▦ *Less than 15 minutes to prepare*

1½ cups cold milk
1 package (4-serving) ☆ Jell-O
    instant pudding—
    vanilla flavor

1 container (4½ oz.) Cool Whip
    non-dairy whipped
    topping, thawed
½ cup frozen concentrate for
    orange juice

• Combine milk and pudding mix in bowl. Beat slowly with rotary beater or at lowest speed of electric mixer until blended, about 2 minutes. Blend in whipped topping. Measure 1 cup of mixture and blend in concentrate. Spoon mixtures alternately into 4-ounce paper cups. Draw wooden stick through to marble and leave inserted in center for handle. Freeze until firm, about 4 hours. Makes 8 pops.

BANANA YOGURT FREEZE

Nutritious and a welcome treat for any snack occasion

▦ *Less than 15 minutes to prepare*

1½ cups cold milk
1 package (4-serving) ☆ Jell-O
    instant pudding—
    vanilla flavor
1 container (8 oz.) plain
    yogurt

2 bananas, mashed
1 teaspoon rum extract
    (optional)
1 cup thawed Cool Whip
    non-dairy
    whipped topping

• Combine milk, pudding mix and yogurt in deep narrow-bottom bowl. Beat at lowest speed of electric mixer for 2 minutes. Blend in bananas, extract and whipped topping. Pour into paper baking cups or 4-ounce paper cups, inserting wooden sticks, if desired. Freeze until firm, about 4 hours.
• Remove from cups and roll in toasted flaked coconut, if desired. Makes 8 servings. NOTE: To serve as dessert, spoon mixture into individual parfait glasses. Garnish with additional thawed whipped topping and freeze until firm. Garnish with whole or sliced strawberries or maraschino cherries, if desired.

PUDDING CONES

▦ *Less than 15 minutes to prepare*

1 package (4-serving) ☆ Jell-O
    instant pudding—
    vanilla or chocolate
    flavor*
1½ cups cold milk

1 cup thawed Cool Whip non-
    dairy whipped topping
¼ cup chopped nuts or
    peanuts
5 ice cream wafer cones

*Or use ★ Jell-O pudding—chocolate flavor

• Prepare pudding mix as directed on package for pudding using 1½ cups milk. (If using cooked pudding, pour into bowl and chill.) Blend in whipped topping and nuts. Chill.
• Just before serving, spoon pudding mixture into wafer cups. Garnish with additional whipped topping and nuts or assorted candies or maraschino cherries, if desired. Makes 5 servings.
NOTE: To make pudding mixture thick enough to <u>scoop</u> into wafer cones, reduce milk to 1 cup and prepare as directed.

FROZEN PUDDING SANDWICHES

Keep these on hand in your freezer for special snack times

🕐 *From 15 to 30 minutes to prepare*

1 ½ cups cold milk
½ cup creamy or chunky
peanut butter

1 package (4-serving) ☆ Jell-O
instant pudding — vanilla or
chocolate flavor
24 graham crackers or chocolate
wafers

- *Add milk gradually to peanut butter in deep narrow-bottom bowl, blending until smooth. Add pudding mix. Beat slowly with rotary beater or at lowest speed of electric mixer until well blended, about 2 minutes. Let stand 5 minutes.*
- *Spread filling about ½ inch thick on 12 of the crackers. Top with remaining crackers, pressing lightly and smoothing around edges with spatula. Freeze until firm, about 3 hours. Wrap individual sandwiches for storage. Makes 12 sandwiches.*

BUTTERSCOTCH-TOP COFFEE CAKE

Make two at once...great for your next a.m.'club meeting

Over 30 minutes to prepare

1 package (13 ¾ oz.) hot roll mix
1 package (4-serving) ★ Jell-O
   pudding — butterscotch flavor
½ cup firmly packed dark brown sugar

¼ cup butter or margarine
½ cup sour cream
¼ cup Baker's Angel Flake
   coconut or chopped nuts

• Prepare hot roll mix as directed on package. Let rise in warm place until doubled in bulk, about 30 minutes. Divide dough in half. Press into two lightly greased 9-inch layer pans. Let rise another 30 minutes.

• Combine pudding mix and brown sugar. Cut in butter until mixture is crumbly. Stir in sour cream. With finger or back of spoon, press holes in dough about 1 inch apart. Spoon pudding mixture over dough. Sprinkle with coconut or chopped nuts. Bake at 375° for 25 to 30 minutes. Serve warm, or heat before serving.

BUTTER PECAN CRUMB CAKE

Over 30 minutes to prepare

½ cup firmly packed brown sugar
½ cup all-purpose flour
½ teaspoon cinnamon
¼ cup butter or margarine,
   softened
1 package (2-layer) yellow
   cake mix or pudding-
   included cake mix

1 package (4-serving) ☆ Jell-O
   instant pudding —
   butter pecan flavor
1 cup (½ pint) sour cream
⅓ cup oil
4 eggs
½ teaspoon maple extract
   (optional)

• Combine brown sugar, flour and cinnamon in small bowl. Cut in butter with pastry blender or two knives to make crumbs. Set aside.

• Combine remaining ingredients in large mixer bowl. Blend, then beat at medium speed for 4 minutes. Pour into greased and floured 10-inch tube pan. Bake at 350° for 50 minutes. Carefully remove <u>partially baked</u> cake from oven and sprinkle immediately with reserved crumb mixture. Bake 10 to 15 minutes longer or until cake tester inserted in center comes out clean and cake begins to pull away from sides of pan. <u>Do not underbake.</u> Cool in pan 10 minutes. Carefully remove from pan; turn crumb side up and finish cooling on rack.

HOMEMADE ICE CREAM SAUCES...

Ice cream becomes a very special snack-time treat when you add one of these thick and luscious sauces...all easy to make!

QUICK ICE CREAM SAUCE

Less than 15 minutes to prepare

1 package (4-serving) ☆ Jell-O
   instant pudding — butterscotch,
   chocolate or chocolate
   fudge flavor

¾ cup light corn syrup
¾ cup evaporated milk or
   light cream

• Combine pudding mix and corn syrup in bowl. Gradually add evaporated milk, stirring constantly. Let stand 10 minutes. Serve over ice cream or cake. Store, covered, in refrigerator for up to a week. Makes about 2 cups.

CHOCOLATE ICE CREAM SAUCE

Less than 15 minutes to prepare

1 package (4-serving) ★ Jell-O
pudding—chocolate, milk chocolate
or chocolate fudge flavor
1½ cups water

½ cup sugar
½ square Baker's brand
unsweetened chocolate
1 tablespoon butter or margarine

• Combine pudding mix, water, sugar and chocolate in saucepan. Cook and stir until mixture comes to a boil. Remove from heat. Add butter. Serve warm or cold on cake or ice cream. (If sauce becomes thick, thin with water.) Makes 2 cups.

EASY PUDDING MILK SHAKE

Less than 15 minutes to prepare

4 cups cold milk
1 package (4-serving) ☆ Jell-O
instant pudding— any flavor

4 scoops ice cream—any
flavor (optional)

• Pour 2 cups of milk into bowl or 2-quart shaker or jar with tight-fitting cover. Add pudding mix. Beat slowly with rotary beater or at lowest speed of electric mixer until blended, about 2 minutes, <u>or</u> cover shaker tightly and shake vigorously until blended, about 30 seconds. Add remaining milk and the ice cream. Beat or shake until thoroughly mixed. Serve at once. Makes 6 servings with ice cream or 4 without.

PEANUT BUTTER COOKIES

Kids— and grown-ups, too— go for the peanut flavor of these homemade crisps

Over 30 minutes to prepare·

1 cup unsifted all-purpose flour
½ teaspoon baking soda
⅛ teaspoon salt
⅓ cup butter, margarine or
vegetable shortening

½ cup creamy or chunky
peanut butter
1 package (4-serving) ☆ Jell-O
instant pudding— vanilla flavor
1 egg

- Mix flour with baking soda and salt.
- Cream butter. Blend in peanut butter and pudding mix. Add egg and beat until light and fluffy. Gradually add flour mixture, beating after each addition until smooth. Shape dough into small balls and place on greased baking sheets. Flatten balls with fork. Bake at 375° for 10 to 12 minutes, or until lightly browned. Cool on racks. Makes 2½ dozen.

QUICK CHIP COOKIES

Easy homemade drop cookies start with a pair of mixes

🥫 *From 15 to 30 minutes to prepare*

1 package (4-serving) ★ Jell-O
   pudding— vanilla flavor*
1 cup all-purpose biscuit mix
2 tablespoons sugar
¼ cup oil

1 egg, slightly beaten
3 tablespoons water
½ cup Baker's brand chocolate
   flavor baking chips

    * Or use ☆ Jell-O instant pudding and eliminate sugar

• Combine pudding mix, biscuit mix and sugar in bowl. Add oil, egg and water.
Blend well. Stir in chips. Drop from teaspoon onto ungreased baking sheets.
Bake at 375° for about 12 minutes, or until lightly browned. Remove from
baking sheets and cool on racks. Store in tightly covered container. Makes
about 2 to 2½ dozen.

CHEWY BROWNIES

Moist and fudgy, and simple to make any time

🥫 *Over 30 minutes to prepare*

1 package (4-serving) ★ Jell-O
   pudding— chocolate fudge,
   chocolate or milk
   chocolate flavor*
½ cup unsifted all-purpose flour
¼ teaspoon Calumet baking powder

⅓ cup butter or margarine
⅔ cup sugar
2 eggs
1 teaspoon vanilla
½ cup chopped walnuts

    * Or use ☆ Jell-O instant pudding and reduce flour to ⅓ cup

• Combine pudding mix, flour and baking powder and mix well.
• Melt butter in saucepan. Remove from heat and add sugar. Beat in eggs, one at
a time. Blend in pudding mixture and vanilla. Stir in nuts. Spread onto greased
8-inch square pan. Bake at 350° for 35 minutes. (Or use 9-inch pan and bake
30 minutes.) Cool in pan, then cut into bars. Makes about 18 bars.

COCONUT BUTTERSCOTCH CRISPS

Make these ahead for a lunchbox or after-school homemade treat

🥫 *Over 30 minutes to prepare*

1½ cups unsifted all-purpose
   flour
½ teaspoon baking soda
½ cup butter or other shortening
½ cup firmly packed brown sugar

1 package (4-serving) ★ Jell-O
   pudding— butterscotch flavor
1 egg
½ cup Baker's Angel Flake or
   cookie coconut

• Mix flour with baking soda. Cream butter and beat in sugar and pudding mix.
Add egg and blend well. Stir in flour mixture. Form into small balls about 1 inch
in diameter. (Flour hands lightly, if necessary.) Roll in coconut. Place on ungreased
baking sheets and press with bottom of glass that has been dipped in flour. Bake at
350° for 10 minutes. Remove from baking sheets and cool on racks. (These can
be wrapped in aluminum foil and frozen or stored at room temperature.)
Makes about 3 dozen cookies.

PISTACHIO-COCONUT COOKIES

Crisp drop cookies with chewy centers, a welcome blend of flavors

📖 Over 30 minutes to prepare

1 package (2-layer) white cake mix
1 package (4-serving) ☆ Jell-O
   instant pudding—
   pistachio flavor
½ cup oil

3 tablespoons water
2 eggs
½ cup chopped nuts
½ cup Baker's Angel Flake
   coconut

- Combine all ingredients in bowl. Blend well. Drop from teaspoon onto greased baking sheets. Bake at 350° for about 10 minutes or until lightly browned around edges. Store in tightly covered container. Makes 6 dozen.

CHEWY MACAROONS

Whip them up in minutes...they're chewy and yummy!

📖 From 15 to 30 minutes to prepare

1 package (4-serving) ★ Jell-O
   pudding—vanilla flavor
2⅔ cups (about) Baker's Angel
   Flake coconut

⅔ cup sweetened condensed milk
½ teaspoon almond extract
Diced maraschino cherries
   (optional)

- Combine pudding mix, coconut, milk and extract. Drop from teaspoon onto well greased and floured baking sheets. Garnish with cherries. Bake at 325° for 12 to 15 minutes or until edges are golden brown. Remove from baking sheets at <u>once</u> and cool thoroughly on racks. For ease in removing cookies from baking sheet, dip spatula in water. (If cookies cool and become difficult to remove, reheat in oven for a few minutes.) Makes 2½ dozen.

QUICK LEMON CRISPS

Turn these out from ingredients on hand, in just minutes

📖 Over 30 minutes to prepare

1¾ cups unsifted
   all-purpose flour
¾ teaspoon baking soda
   Dash of salt
¾ cup vegetable shortening

1 cup sugar
2 packages (4-serving) ☆ Jell-O
   instant pudding—
   lemon flavor
3 eggs

- Mix flour with soda and salt. Cream shortening. Add sugar and pudding mix and continue beating until light and fluffy. Add eggs and mix thoroughly. Add flour mixture and beat until well blended. Drop by teaspoonfuls onto greased baking sheets, about 2 inches apart. Bake at 375° for 8 to 10 minutes. Store in tightly covered container. Makes 5 dozen cookies.

BUTTERSCOTCH BONBONS

Rolled oats, coconut and nuts team to make these quick delicious candies

▮ From 15 to 30 minutes to prepare

3 cups quick-cooking rolled oats
1 cup Baker's Angel Flake
   coconut
½ cup coarsely chopped nuts
1 cup sugar

1 package (4-serving) ★ Jell-O
   pudding or ☆ Jell-O instant
   pudding—butterscotch flavor
½ cup milk
½ cup butter or margarine

• Combine oats, coconut and nuts in large bowl. Blend sugar, pudding mix, milk and butter in heavy saucepan. Bring to a boil. Reduce heat and boil 1 minute, stirring constantly. Pour over oat mixture and mix well. Drop from teaspoon onto wax paper on baking sheets. (If mixture becomes dry, add small amount of milk or cream.) Chill 15 to 20 minutes until set. Store in refrigerator. Makes about 5½ dozen candies.

PUDDING PRALINES

Easy homemade candies, just like those New Orleans confections

▮ Over 30 minutes to prepare

1 package (4-serving) ★ Jell-O
   pudding—butterscotch,
   chocolate, chocolate fudge
   or vanilla flavor
1 cup granulated sugar

½ cup firmly packed brown sugar
⅔ cup evaporated milk
2 tablespoons butter
   or margarine
1½ cups pecan halves or pieces

•Combine pudding mix, sugars, milk and butter in saucepan. Cook and stir over low heat until sugar dissolves and mixture comes to a boil. Continue to boil gently, stirring often, until a small amount of syrup forms a very soft ball in cold water (or to a temperature of 230°). Remove from heat. Add nuts. Beat for 2 minutes. Quickly drop from tablespoon onto wax paper, making each praline about 2 inches in diameter. Let stand until firm. Makes about 2 dozen.

EASY FUDGE

An easy short-cut way to great fudge

▮ From 15 to 30 minutes to prepare

1 package (4-serving) ★ Jell-O
   pudding— chocolate,
   chocolate fudge or
   milk chocolate flavor

¼ cup milk
2 tablespoons butter or margarine
2 cups confectioners sugar
¼ cup chopped nuts

•Combine pudding mix and milk in saucepan. Add butter and bring to a boil over medium heat, stirring constantly. Remove from heat. Stir in sugar and beat until smooth. Add nuts. Quickly pour into greased or wax paper-lined 8x4-inch loaf pan. Chill until firm, about 30 minutes. Cut into pieces. Store, covered, in refrigerator. Makes about 18 large pieces.

Good Old-Fashioned Desserts

They're part of our tradition— desserts like these. Each comes with its own special memory. The Pineapple Upside-Down Cake your mother used to make for church socials. The Coconut Custard Pie your uncle insisted on having along with the pumpkin for Thanksgiving. The Ambrosia pudding you always had when you visited your Southern cousins. Grandmother's beautiful Floating Island. The Apple Crisp that made October special.

There's a lot of nostalgia— and a lot of memorable dessert eating — wrapped up in these old-fashioned desserts. Now pudding is the keystone, the building block that takes the work out of making them, while still recapturing all those marvelous old-fashioned tastes. Here, one of the most memorable of all, Lemon Cheesecake— creamy and luscious, an American classic.

LEMON CHEESECAKE

 *Over 30 minutes to prepare*

1¼ cups graham cracker crumbs	4 cups cold milk
3 tablespoons sugar	2 packages (4-serving) ☆ Jell-O
⅓ cup butter or margarine	instant pudding—
2 packages (8 oz. each)	lemon flavor
cream cheese, softened	

- Combine crumbs, sugar and butter and mix well. Press mixture firmly on bottom and on sides (to within 1 inch of top) of 9-or 10-inch springform pan (or use 9-inch square pan; press mixture on bottom). Bake at 350°about 8 minutes or until lightly browned. Cool.
- Beat cream cheese in large bowl until smooth. Gradually add 1 cup of the milk, blending until mixture is very smooth. Add remaining milk and pudding mix. Beat with rotary beater just until well blended, about 1 minute. Pour carefully into crumb-lined pan. Chill until firm, about 3 hours. Garnish with whipped topping and quartered lemon slices, if desired.

APPLESAUCE-SPICE CAKE

Rich and spicy, with the nostalgic tang of autumn apples

🧂 *Over 30 minutes to prepare*

1 package (2-layer) yellow
   cake mix
1 package (4-serving) ☆ Jell-O
   instant pudding—
   vanilla flavor
4 eggs
1 cup applesauce

½ cup water
¼ cup oil
½ teaspoon cinnamon
½ teaspoon nutmeg
¼ teaspoon allspice (optional)
½ cup raisins, finely
   chopped (optional)

• Combine all ingredients in large mixer bowl. Blend, then beat at medium speed of electric mixer for 4 minutes. Pour into greased and floured 10-inch tube or fluted tube pan. Bake at 350° for 50 to 55 minutes or until cake tester inserted in center comes out clean and cake begins to pull away from sides of pan. <u>Do not underbake.</u> Cool in pan 15 minutes. Remove from pan and finish cooling on rack.

RAISIN-NUT POUND CAKE

Pudding plus yogurt gives a new richness to this old favorite

🧂 *Over 30 minutes to prepare*

1 package (2-layer) yellow
   cake mix or pudding-
   included cake mix
1 package (4-serving) ☆ Jell-O
   instant pudding—
   vanilla flavor
1 container (8 oz.) plain yogurt

⅓ cup oil
4 eggs
¼ cup finely chopped nuts
¼ cup finely chopped raisins
¼ cup finely chopped
   mixed candied
   fruit (optional)

• Combine all ingredients in large mixer bowl. Blend, then beat at medium speed of electric mixer for 4 minutes. Pour into two 9x5-inch loaf pans which have been lined with paper on bottoms. Bake at 350° for 40 to 45 minutes, or until cake tester inserted in centers comes out clean and cake begins to pull away from sides of pan. <u>Do not underbake.</u> Cool in pans 15 minutes. Remove from pans and finish cooling on racks.

MARBLE CAKE

 🧂 *Over 30 minutes to prepare*

1 package (2-layer) yellow cake mix
1 package (4-serving) ☆ Jell-O
   instant pudding—vanilla flavor
4 eggs
1 cup water

¼ cup oil
1 package (4-serving) ☆ Jell-O
   instant pudding—chocolate
   or chocolate fudge flavor
¼ cup water

• Combine cake mix, vanilla pudding mix, eggs, 1 cup water and oil in large mixer bowl. Blend, then beat at medium speed of electric mixer for 4 minutes. Spoon one-third of batter into bowl. Blend in chocolate pudding mix and ¼ cup water.
• Pour half the vanilla batter into greased and floured 10-inch fluted tube pan. Add half the chocolate batter. Repeat layers. Bake at 350° for 45 to 50 minutes or until cake tester inserted in center comes out clean and cake begins to pull away from sides of pan. <u>Do not underbake.</u> Cool in pan about 15 minutes. Remove from pan and finish cooling on rack.

PEACH UPSIDE-DOWN CAKE

Especially rich, this version with the plus of sour cream

Over 30 minutes to prepare

¼ cup butter or margarine,
   melted
⅓ cup firmly packed light
   brown sugar
1 can (29 oz.) sliced peaches,
   well drained
1 package (2-layer) yellow
   cake mix or pudding-
   included cake mix

1 package (4-serving) ☆ Jell-O
   instant pudding—
   vanilla flavor
4 eggs
1 cup (½ pt.) sour cream
¼ cup oil
½ teaspoon almond extract
   (optional)

- Combine butter and brown sugar. Pour into 13x9-inch pan. Arrange peaches in rows on sugar mixture.
- Combine remaining ingredients in large mixer bowl. Blend, then beat at medium speed of electric mixer for 4 minutes. Spoon carefully over peach slices in pan. Bake at 350° for 50 to 55 minutes or until cake springs back when lightly touched. Cool in pan for 5 minutes. Invert onto serving platter and remove pan. Serve warm or cool with whipped topping, if desired.

GLAZED PINEAPPLE UPSIDE-DOWN CAKE

Pudding adds a new lustrous sheen to the pineapple topping

🥫 Over 30 minutes to prepare

1 can (20 oz.) sliced pineapple
   in juice
1 package (4-serving) ★ Jell-O
   pudding or ☆ Jell-O
   instant pudding —
   vanilla flavor
10 maraschino cherries
½ cup firmly packed brown sugar

1 package (2-layer) yellow
   cake mix
1 package (4-serving) ☆ Jell-O
   instant pudding —
   vanilla flavor
4 eggs
1 cup water
¼ cup oil

- Drain pineapple, reserving juice. Combine pudding mix and pineapple juice and set aside Arrange pineapple slices in bottom of 13x9-inch baking pan. Place cherry in center of each. Pour pudding mixture over pineapple. Sprinkle with brown sugar.
- Combine cake mix, pudding mix, eggs, water and oil in large mixer bowl. Blend, then beat at medium speed of electric mixer for 4 minutes. Pour over pineapple topping mixture in pan. Bake at 350° for 55 to 60 minutes or until top springs back when lightly pressed. Cool 5 minutes in pan. then invert on serving platter and let stand 1 minute before removing pan. Serve warm with whipped topping, if desired.

EASY BOSTON CREAM PIE

This simplified version goes together in a jiffy

🥫 Over 30 minutes to prepare

1 package (6-serving) ★ Jell-O
   pudding — vanilla or
   banana cream flavor
2 ⅓ cups milk
1 square Baker's
   unsweetened chocolate

1 tablespoon butter or
   margarine
½ cup thawed Cool Whip
   non-dairy whipped
   topping
1 baked 8-or 9-inch
   yellow cake layer,
   cooled

- Combine pudding mix and milk in saucepan. Cook and stir over medium heat until mixture comes to a <u>full</u> boil. Remove from heat. Measure 1 cup pudding into bowl. Add chocolate and butter and stir until melted. Cover both pudding surfaces with plastic wrap and chill.
- Beat chilled vanilla pudding just until smooth. Fold in whipped topping. Split cake layer in half horizontally to make 2 layers. Place 1 cake layer on serving plate, spread with vanilla pudding mixture and top with second layer. Beat chilled chocolate-flavored pudding until smooth and creamy. Spread over cake. Chill at least 1 hour. Makes 6 to 8 servings.

EASY BLACK-BOTTOM PIE

Chocolate chips plus pudding...what could be easier?

🔲 *Over 30 minutes to prepare*

1 unbaked 9-inch pie shell
½ cup Baker's chocolate flavor
baking chips

1 package (6-serving) ☆ Jell-O
instant pudding — vanilla
or banana cream flavor*

2½ cups milk

* *Or use ★ Jell-O pudding, any flavor except lemon, and use 2¾ cups milk*

• *Bake pie shell at 450° for 12 to 15 minutes, or until lightly browned. Remove from oven. Immediately sprinkle chips in single layer on bottom of pie shell. Let stand 3 to 5 minutes to melt chips, then spread over bottom of crust. Cool thoroughly.*
• *Prepare pudding mix as directed on package for pie. Pour into chocolate-coated crust. (If using cooked pudding, cover surface with plastic wrap.) Chill 3 hours (4 for cooked). Garnish with whipped topping and chocolate curls, if desired.*

FROZEN BLACK-BOTTOM PIE

Cool and creamy, a new way with an old favorite

🔲 *Over 30 minutes to prepare*

1 package (6-serving) ★ Jell-O
pudding — any flavor
except lemon
2 cups milk
1½ to 2 tablespoons chocolate
syrup

1 baked 9-inch pie shell,
cooled
1 container (4½ oz.)
Cool Whip non-dairy
whipped topping,
thawed

• *Combine pudding mix and milk in saucepan. Cook and stir over medium heat until mixture comes to a full bubbling boil. Remove from heat and cool 5 minutes, stirring twice. Add syrup to ½ cup of the filling; pour into pie shell and chill. Cover remaining mixture with plastic wrap and chill.*
• *Beat chilled mixture until creamy. Blend in half of the whipped topping. Spoon into pie shell and freeze until firm, about 4 hours. Garnish with remaining topping.*

FLUFFY BANANA CREAM PIE

Make the classic banana cream pie by using ★ Jell-O pudding,
following package directions and slicing bananas into the pie shell before filling.
Or try this fluffy — even quicker — version.

🔲 *Less than 15 minutes to prepare*

1 envelope Dream Whip
whipped topping mix*
1 banana
1 baked 9-inch pie shell, cooled

1 package (6-serving) ☆ Jell-O
instant pudding — banana
cream or vanilla flavor
2 cups cold milk

* *Or use 1 container (4½ oz.) Cool Whip non-dairy whipped topping, thawed*

• *Prepare whipped topping mix as directed on package.*
• *Slice banana into pie shell.*
• *Combine pudding mix and milk in bowl. Beat slowly with rotary beater or at lowest speed of electric mixer for 1 minute. Fold in half of the prepared whipped topping. Pour filling over banana in pie shell. Chill at least 1 hour. Garnish with remaining whipped topping.*

SPECIAL LEMON MERINGUE PIE

A universal favorite, made even better this way

🍴 *From 15 to 30 minutes to prepare*

1 package (4-serving) ★ Jell-O
    pudding—lemon flavor
²/₃ cup sugar
2 ¼ cups water
3 egg yolks

2 tablespoons lemon juice
2 tablespoons butter or margarine
1 baked 9-inch pie shell, cooled
3 egg whites
6 tablespoons sugar

- Combine pudding mix, ²/₃ cup sugar and ¼ cup of the water in saucepan. Blend in egg yolks and remaining water. Cook and stir over medium heat, until mixture comes to a <u>full bubbling boil.</u> Remove from heat. Blend in lemon juice and butter. Cool 5 minutes, stirring twice. Pour into pie shell.
- Beat egg whites until foamy throughout. Gradually beat in 6 tablespoons sugar and continue beating until mixture will form stiff shiny peaks. Spread over pie filling, sealing well at edges. Bake at 425° for 5 to 10 minutes or until meringue is delicately browned. Cool at least 4 hours before cutting.

KEY LIME PIE

A light fluffy variation of the famous Florida pie

From 15 to 30 minutes to prepare

1 package (4-serving) ★ Jell-O
    pudding — lemon flavor
1 cup sugar
1½ cups water
2 egg yolks
3 tablespoons lime juice

¾ teaspoon grated lime rind
2 egg whites
¼ cup sugar
    Green food coloring
1 baked 9-inch graham cracker
    crumb crust or pie shell, cooled

• Combine pudding mix, 1 cup sugar and ¼ cup of the water in saucepan. Blend in egg yolks. Add remaining water. Cook and stir over medium heat until mixture comes to a *full bubbling boil.* Remove from heat. Stir in lime juice and rind.

• Beat egg whites until foamy throughout. Gradually add ¼ cup sugar and continue beating until mixture will form stiff shiny peaks. Blend in pie filling mixture. Add enough food coloring to tint light green. Pour into crust. Chill until firm. Garnish with whipped topping and lime twists or slices, if desired.

DEEP-DISH APPLE PIE

Pudding adds to the special old-fashioned flavor of this classic

Over 30 minutes to prepare

5 cups thinly sliced peeled
    apples
1½ cups water
¼ cup sugar
1 tablespoon lemon juice

1 package (6-serving) ★ Jell-O
    pudding — vanilla flavor
½ teaspoon cinnamon
1 tablespoon butter or margarine
    Pastry for 1-crust pie

• Combine apples, water, sugar, lemon juice, pudding mix and cinnamon in 2-quart baking dish. Dot with butter.

• Roll pastry to fit top of dish. Place over apple mixture. Flute edges and cut several slits near center. Bake at 425° for 45 minutes or until crust is lightly browned. Serve with ice cream or whipped topping, if desired.

COCONUT CUSTARD PIE

This rich golden favorite is now easy to make

Over 30 minutes to prepare

1 package (4½ oz.)* Jell-O
    Americana golden egg
    custard mix
2¾ cups milk
1 egg yolk (optional)

⅔ cup Baker's Angel Flake
    coconut
1 baked 9-or 10-inch pie
    shell, cooled
    Ground nutmeg (optional)

Or use 3-ounce package, 2 cups milk and 8-inch pie shell

• Blend custard mix with milk in saucepan. Add egg yolk. Bring quickly to a boil, stirring constantly. Remove from heat. Cool 30 minutes, stirring often.

• Sprinkle coconut in pie shell. Carefully pour in custard mixture. Sprinkle with nutmeg and additional flaked coconut, toasted, if desired. Chill until set, at least 4 hours. Refrigerate any leftover pie.

PUMPKIN PIE

Two recipes for rich creamy pumpkin pie— both easy, one with no cooking

Less than 15 minutes for instant pudding, over 30 minutes for cooked

1 package (6-serving) ★ Jell-O
   pudding or ☆ Jell-O instant
   pudding— vanilla flavor
1½ cups milk
   1 cup canned pumpkin

1 teaspoon pumpkin pie spice
1 cup thawed Cool Whip non-
   dairy whipped topping
1 baked 9-inch pie shell,
   cooled

• *If using* ★ *Jell-O pudding:* Combine pudding mix, milk, pumpkin and spice in saucepan. Cook and stir over medium heat until mixture comes to *full bubbling boil*. Remove from heat and cool 5 minutes, stirring twice. Cover with plastic wrap and chill. Fold in whipped topping and pour into pie shell. Chill 3 hours. Garnish with additional whipped topping, if desired.

• *If using* ☆ *Jell-O instant pudding:* Combine pudding mix, milk, pumpkin, spice and whipped topping in deep narrow-bottom bowl. Beat at low speed of electric mixer for 1 minute. Pour into pie shell. Chill until set, at least 3 hours. Garnish with additional whipped topping, if desired.

PECAN PIE

It started in the South...now it's a favorite everywhere

Over 30 minutes to prepare

1 package (4-serving) ☆ Jell-O
   instant pudding— vanilla or
   butterscotch flavor
1 cup light or dark corn syrup

¾ cup evaporated milk
1 egg, slightly beaten
1 cup chopped pecans
1 unbaked 8-inch pie shell

• Blend pudding mix with corn syrup. Gradually add evaporated milk and egg, blending well. Add pecans and pour into pie shell. Bake at 375° until top is firm and just begins to crack, about 45 to 50 minutes. Cool at least 3 hours before cutting. Garnish with whipped topping and additional pecans, if desired.

CREAMY SWEET POTATO PIE

Another Southern classic, now easy to make like this

From 15 to 30 minutes to prepare

1 can (15 oz.) sweet potatoes
1 package (4-serving) ★ Jell-O
   pudding— vanilla flavor
2 tablespoons sugar
½ teaspoon cinnamon

½ teaspoon ginger
½ teaspoon nutmeg
1½ cups milk
1 baked 9-inch pie shell,
   cooled

• Drain sweet potatoes, reserving ¼ cup liquid. Mash, then add reserved liquid.

• Combine pudding mix, sugar, spices, milk and sweet potatoes in saucepan. Cook and stir over medium heat until mixture comes to a *full bubbling boil*. Remove from heat. Cool 5 minutes, stirring once or twice. Pour into pie shell. Chill. Garnish with whipped topping and a sprinkle of nutmeg, if desired.

CHARLOTTE

Tradition calls for ladyfingers but you can use pound cake slices, if you prefer

▯ *Over 30 minutes to prepare*

1 package (4-serving) ★ Jell-O
   pudding— chocolate,
   coconut cream, vanilla or
   French vanilla flavor*
2 cups milk
6 ladyfingers

¼ cup strawberry jam
1 envelope Dream Whip
   whipped topping mix
1 teaspoon lemon rind
   (omit if using chocolate or
   coconut cream flavors)

Or use ☆ Jell-O instant pudding

• Prepare pudding mix with milk as directed on package. Cover surface with plastic wrap and chill 2 hours. (If using instant pudding, don't chill.)
• Split ladyfingers. Spread with jam and press together. Cut each in half crosswise.
• Prepare whipped topping mix as directed on package. Blend 1 cup into chilled pudding. Add lemon rind. Spoon about half of pudding mixture into shallow 1-quart glass bowl. Line sides with filled ladyfinger halves. Spoon in remaining pudding mixture. Chill. Before serving, top with remaining whipped topping. Garnish with toasted almond halves or toasted flaked coconut, if desired. Makes 6 servings.

FLOATING ISLAND

An elegant turn-of-the-century dessert, simplified now, but just as delicious

▯ *Over 30 minutes to prepare*

1 package (3 oz.) Jell-O
   Americana golden egg
   custard mix
3 cups milk

2 egg yolks, slightly beaten
1 teaspoon vanilla
2 egg whites
¼ cup sugar

• Combine custard mix and 1 cup of the milk in saucepan. Blend in yolks. Add remaining milk. Bring mixture quickly to a boil, stirring constantly. Remove from heat. Stir in vanilla. Cover with plastic wrap and cool about 30 minutes. Stir and pour into serving dish. Chill.
• Beat egg whites until foamy throughout. Gradually add sugar and continue beating until mixture forms soft peaks. Drop from tablespoon onto ungreased baking sheet, making 6 meringues. Broil until lightly browned. Stir chilled custard. Place meringues on top of custard. Makes 6 servings.

AMBROSIA PUDDING

Just creamy pudding, fruit and coconut...heavenly!

▯ *Less than 15 minutes to prepare*

1 package (4-serving) ☆ Jell-O
   instant pudding— lemon
   or vanilla flavor*
2 cups cold milk

½ teaspoon grated orange rind (optional)
½ cup diced fresh orange sections
   (or drained canned mandarin
   orange sections)
⅔ cup Baker's Angel Flake coconut

Or use ★ Jell-O pudding— banana cream flavor

• Prepare pudding mix with milk as directed on package for pudding.(If using cooked pudding, cover with plastic wrap and chill.)Fold in orange rind, orange sections and coconut. Pour into dessert dishes or serving bowl and chill. Makes 6 servings.

BREAD PUDDING

Hearty old-fashioned dessert, now ready in minutes

From 15 to 30 minutes to prepare

1 package (4-serving) ★ Jell-O
pudding — vanilla flavor
2 tablespoons sugar
3 cups milk
¼ cup raisins
1 tablespoon butter or margarine

½ teaspoon vanilla
6 slices dry white bread, cut
in ¾-inch cubes
2 tablespoons sugar
¼ teaspoon cinnamon
⅛ teaspoon nutmeg

- *Combine pudding mix and 2 tablespoons sugar in saucepan. Blend in 2 cups of the milk. Add raisins. Cook and stir over medium heat until mixture comes to a <u>full</u> boil. Remove from heat and stir in butter and vanilla. Pour remaining milk over bread cubes in bowl to moisten, then stir into pudding mixture. Pour into 1-quart baking dish.*
- *Combine 2 tablespoons sugar and spices. Sprinkle over pudding. Broil until sugar is lightly browned and bubbly, about 4 or 5 minutes. Serve warm or chilled. Makes 6 servings.*

INSTANT BREAD PUDDING

Old-fashioned, but quicker than ever this way

▤ *Less than 15 minutes to prepare*

4 or 5 slices white bread	⅛ teaspoon nutmeg
1 package (4-serving) ☆ Jell-O	⅛ teaspoon cinnamon
instant pudding—	½ teaspoon vanilla
vanilla flavor	1 tablespoon brown sugar
2 cups cold milk	2 tablespoons
⅛ teaspoon salt	chopped nuts

- Trim crusts from bread. Toast, then cut into ½-inch cubes. Arrange half of bread cubes in bottom of 1-quart baking dish.
- Combine pudding mix, milk, salt, spices and vanilla in bowl. Beat slowly with rotary beater or at lowest speed of electric mixer until well blended, about 2 minutes. Pour half the pudding over bread cubes. Add remaining bread cubes and top with remaining pudding. Combine brown sugar and nuts and sprinkle over pudding. Broil 2 to 3 minutes. Chill. Makes 5 or 6 servings.

SOUTHERN BANANA PUDDING

Really special, with vanilla water crust, creamy vanilla filling, fluffy meringue topping

▤ *From 15 to 30 minutes to prepare*

1 package (4-serving) ★ Jell-O	25 vanilla wafers
pudding— vanilla or	2 large bananas, sliced
banana cream flavor	2 egg whites
2 egg yolks	Dash of salt
2½ cups milk	¼ cup sugar

- Combine pudding mix, egg yolks and milk in saucepan. Cook and stir over medium heat until mixture comes to a <u>full</u> boil. Remove from heat.
- Arrange layer of vanilla wafers on bottom and sides of 1½-quart baking dish Add a layer of banana slices and of pudding. Continue layering wafers, banana slices and pudding, ending with pudding.
- Beat egg whites with salt until foamy throughout. Gradually beat in sugar and continue beating until mixture will form stiff shiny peaks. Pile lightly on pudding, sealing edges well. Bake at 425° for 5 to 10 minutes or until meringue is lightly browned. Serve warm or chilled. Makes 8 servings.

APPLE CRISP

So easy and delightfully crunchy and tart

▤ *Over 30 minutes to prepare*

4 medium apples, peeled, cored	¼ cup butter or
and sliced (4 cups)	margarine
1 package (4-serving) ★ Jell-O	½ teaspoon cinnamon
pudding— butterscotch	1½ cups Post 40%
flavor	bran flakes

- Combine apple slices and half the pudding mix in greased shallow baking dish.
- Cream butter with remaining pudding mix and cinnamon. Add cereal. Sprinkle over apple mixture. Cover and bake at 375° for 30 minutes or until apples are tender. Serve warm or chilled. Makes 8 servings.

International Favorites

From around the world comes the inspiration for these special desserts. Some are much like the original, but now made simpler, so you can make them without fuss. Some are adaptations of foreign classics, with the same distinctive flavors put in a new easier form. All have the plus of pudding, the dessert-building block that makes the making easy and the results delicious.

You'll find an Easy Tortoni, an Instant Zabaglione, to finish off a dinner with an Italian flourish. A new and easy kind of Pistachio Pie to go with your shish kabobs. Oriental Almond Cream, if you're having Chinese food. Spanish Flan for your paella. Mexican Chocolate Pie for after the chili. But why limit such special desserts like these to international meals only? Any one of them could bring its own welcome flair to any occasion— simple or special. For example, try this super-special Trifle, one of the nicest things the English have ever done for desserts.

ENGLISH TRIFLE

From 15 to 30 minutes to prepare

1 package (4-serving) ★ Jell-O
    pudding— vanilla or
    French vanilla flavor
2½ cups milk
1 baked 8-inch sponge
    cake layer,
    cooled
½ cup orange juice

¼ cup sherry wine (optional)
2 tablespoons water
⅓ cup red raspberry preserves
    or orange marmalade
½ cup soft macaroon crumbs
1 container (4½ oz.) Cool
    Whip non-dairy whipped
    topping, thawed

• Combine pudding mix and milk in saucepan. Cook and stir over medium heat until mixture comes to a <u>full</u> boil. Cover with plastic wrap and set aside.
• Cut cake into 1½-inch cubes. Place cake cubes in 1- or 1½ -quart serving bowl or in individual serving dishes. Combine orange juice and wine and sprinkle over cake cubes. Add water to preserves and spoon over cake cubes. Top with macaroon crumbs. Spoon in prepared pudding, covering cake completely. Chill at least 2 hours. Top with whipped topping and garnish with toasted almonds and maraschino cherries, if desired. Makes 8 to 10 servings.

CUP OF TRIFLE

Easy enough for everyday dinners, special enough for company

🥛 *From 15 to 30 minutes to prepare*

1½ cups ½-inch pound cake
  cubes
2 tablespoons orange juice
  (optional)
3 tablespoons raspberry
  preserves
1 tablespoon water

1 package (4-serving) ☆ Jell-O
  instant pudding — vanilla
  or French vanilla flavor
1½ cups cold milk
1½ cups thawed Cool Whip
  non-dairy whipped topping
1 tablespoon sherry wine
  (optional)

- Arrange cake cubes in bottom of each serving glass. Sprinkle with orange juice. Combine raspberry preserves and water. Spoon over cake cubes.
- Combine pudding mix and milk in bowl. Beat slowly with rotary beater or at lowest speed of electric mixer until well blended, about 2 minutes. Blend in 1 cup of the whipped topping and the sherry. Spoon into glasses. Garnish with remaining whipped topping and maraschino cherries, if desired. Chill. Makes 6 servings.

CRÈME BRÛLÉE

From France, this rich, melt-in-the-mouth custard

🥛 *Over 30 minutes to prepare*

1 package (3 oz.) Jell-O
  Americana golden egg
  custard mix
1 cup milk

1 cup heavy cream
1 teaspoon vanilla
¼ cup firmly packed
  brown sugar

- Combine custard mix, milk and cream in saucepan. Bring quickly to a boil, stirring constantly. (Mixture will be thin.) Stir in vanilla. Pour into custard cups, 8-inch pie plate or 1-quart baking dish. Chill until set.
- Sprinkle pudding with brown sugar. Broil in preheated broiler until sugar melts, about 1½ minutes. Chill thoroughly. Serve with thawed frozen fruits, if desired. Makes 4 servings.

CRÈME BRÛLÉE PUDDING

Here's a creamy, easy version of the French classic using pudding

🥛 *Over 30 minutes to prepare*

1 package (6-serving) ★ Jell-O
  pudding — vanilla flavor
1 quart light cream or half
  and half

2 eggs, slightly beaten
1 teaspoon vanilla
¼ cup firmly packed brown
  sugar, sieved

- Combine pudding mix with cream in saucepan, blending well. Cook and stir over medium heat until mixture comes to a <u>full</u> boil. Remove from heat. Stir a small amount of hot mixture into eggs, mixing well. Return to remaining hot mixture and continue cooking over low heat for 1 minute, stirring constantly. Add vanilla and pour into shallow 1½-quart baking dish. Chill at least 3 hours.
- About 15 minutes before serving, sprinkle top evenly with brown sugar. Broil in preheated broiler until sugar melts, about 1½ minutes. Serve over fresh, canned or frozen unsweetened fruit, if desired. Makes 8 servings.

EASY TORTONI

Easy to make, then keep in the freezer for special dessert occasions

📱 *Less than 15 minutes to prepare*

1 package (4-serving) ☆ Jell-O
    instant pudding—
    vanilla flavor
1 envelope Dream Whip whipped
    topping mix

2 tablespoons sugar
1 ¾ cups milk
¼ teaspoon almond extract
½ cup finely chopped nuts or
    macaroon crumbs

• Combine pudding mix, whipped topping mix, sugar, milk and almond extract in deep narrow-bottom mixer bowl. Beat at lowest speed of electric mixer until well blended. Gradually increase beating speed to high and whip until mixture is thick and creamy, about 3 to 5 minutes. Stir in nuts or crumbs, reserving 2 tablespoons for garnish. Spoon into 4-ounce paper soufflé cups. Sprinkle with reserved nuts or crumbs. Freeze until firm, about 3 hours. Makes 6 servings.

CHOCOLATE POT DE CRÈME

Creamy chocolate to serve prettily in little cups, a quick dessert for last-minute guests

📱 *Less than 15 minutes to prepare*

1 package (4-serving) ☆ Jell-O
    instant pudding—
    chocolate flavor

1½ cups cold light cream or
    half and half
½ teaspoon vanilla

• Combine pudding mix, cream and vanilla in bowl. Beat slowly with rotary beater or at lowest speed of electric mixer until well blended, about 2 minutes. Let stand about 5 minutes. Stir until smooth and creamy and spoon into pot de crème cups, custard cups, or individual dessert dishes. Garnish with whipped topping and chocolate curls, if desired. Makes 4 servings.

ORIENTAL ALMOND CREAM

Refreshing finish to a Chinese— or any— dinner

📱 *From 15 to 30 minutes to prepare*

1 package (4-serving) ★ Jell-O
    pudding— vanilla flavor
2 cups milk
2 egg yolks

¼ teaspoon almond extract
2 egg whites,
    stiffly beaten
Fruit topping

• Combine pudding mix and ¼ cup of the milk in saucepan. Blend in egg yolks. Add remaining milk. Cook and stir over medium heat until mixture comes to a <u>full</u> boil. Remove from heat and add extract. Fold mixture gradually into beaten egg whites. Cool, stirring occasionally.
• Spoon into individual dessert glasses or serving bowl. Top with sliced fresh peaches, drained canned fruit cocktail or drained canned mandarin orange sections and chunk pineapple. Add toasted slivered almonds, if desired. Makes 6 servings.

DANISH RICE DESSERT

The Danes might add their cherry liqueur.
This homemade version is very easy, and delicious

🔲 *Over 30 minutes to prepare*

1 package (3 ¾ oz.) Jell-O
Americana rice pudding
1¾ cups milk

¼ cup toasted slivered almonds
½ cup sour cream
Bing cherry sauce

• *Combine rice pudding mix and milk in saucepan. Cook and stir over medium heat until mixture comes to a full boil. Remove from heat and stir in almonds. Cover and chill. Just before serving, fold in sour cream. Serve topped with warm Bing Cherry Sauce. Makes 6 servings.*

BING CHERRY SAUCE: Drain 1 can (16 oz.) pitted dark sweet cherries, reserving syrup. Add water to syrup to make 1½ cups. Combine liquid, 2 tablespoons cornstarch and dash of salt in saucepan. Cook and stir over medium heat until thickened and clear. Remove from heat. Stir in cherries, 1 teaspoon lemon juice and ½ teaspoon almond extract. Serve warm or cool on puddings or cake. Makes 2¼ cups.

RUSSIAN CREAM

A smooth molded dessert, rich with sour cream, wonderful with fruit

🍴 *Over 30 minutes to prepare*

1 package (4-serving) ★ Jell-O pudding— vanilla flavor 2 tablespoons sugar 1 envelope unflavored gelatin	2 cups water 2 cups (1 pt.) sour cream Fruit topping

- Combine pudding mix, sugar and gelatin in saucepan. Add water, blending well. Cook and stir over medium heat until mixture comes to a <u>full</u> boil. Chill until slightly thickened.
- Blend in sour cream, beating until smooth. Pour into 4-cup mold and chill. Unmold and serve with fresh or frozen fruit. Makes 8 servings.

ROTE GRÜTZE

A traditional German dessert, light and luscious, with raspberries and tapioca

🍴 *From 15 to 30 minutes to prepare*

1 package (3¼ oz.) Jell-O Americana vanilla tapioca pudding ¾ cup water	½ cup claret or Burgundy wine 1 package (10 oz.) Birds Eye quick thaw red raspberries

- Combine tapioca pudding mix, water and wine in saucepan. Add frozen raspberries. Cook and stir over medium heat until mixture comes to a <u>full</u> boil and is slightly thickened. Cool 15 to 20 minutes, stirring once or twice. Pour into individual dessert dishes or serving bowl. Chill 3 hours or overnight. Serve with lemon wedges, whipped topping or Basic Custard Sauce (p.15). Makes 4 servings.

SPANISH FLAN WITH SPICED FRUIT

Spain's classic custard, easy now and enhanced with a spicy fruit medley

🍴 *From 15 to 30 minutes to prepare*

1 package (3 oz.) Jell-O Americana golden egg custard mix 2 cups milk 1 egg yolk (optional)	1 can (17 oz.) fruits for salad 1 stick cinnamon 2 whole cloves 2 tablespoons orange juice 1 teaspoon grated orange rind

- Combine custard mix and milk in saucepan. Add egg yolk. Bring quickly to a boil, stirring constantly. Pour into 2½-cup mixing bowl. Chill until set, at least 3 hours.
- Meanwhile, drain fruits, reserving syrup. Bring syrup to a boil with the cinnamon and cloves. Add fruits, orange juice and rind. Chill, then discard spices. To unmold custard, dip in hot water. Serve with the fruit mixture. Makes 4 servings.

ZUPPA INGLESE

The Italian version of the English Trifle

▌ *Over 30 minutes to prepare*

1 package (4-serving) ★ Jell-O
   pudding — vanilla flavor
2 ¼ cups milk
  ¼ cup hot water
  ½ cup apricot or peach preserves
2 teaspoons rum extract

4 slices pound cake
2 tablespoons toasted,
  slivered almonds
1 tablespoon grated Baker's
  German's sweet chocolate
Confectioners sugar

- Combine pudding mix and milk in saucepan. Cook and stir over medium heat until mixture comes to a *full* boil. Remove from heat. Cover with plastic wrap and cool.
- Blend water into preserves. Stir in extract. Cut each cake slice into 4 strips. Arrange around edge of 1-quart serving bowl. Spoon preserves mixture over each strip until cake is saturated. Pour cooled pudding into cake-lined bowl. Chill thoroughly.
- Before serving, sprinkle surface with almonds and chocolate. Garnish with confectioners sugar. Makes 4 to 6 servings.

INSTANT ZABAGLIONE

▌ *From 15 to 30 minutes to prepare*

1 cup cold milk
1½ cups cold light cream or
  half and half
1 package (4-serving) ☆ Jell-O
  instant pudding — vanilla flavor

1 egg white
2 tablespoons sugar
3 tablespoons
  sherry wine

- Pour milk and cream into bowl. Add pudding mix. Beat slowly with rotary beater or at lowest speed of electric mixer until well blended, 1 to 2 minutes. Let stand to set, about 5 minutes.
- Meanwhile, beat egg white until foamy throughout. Gradually add sugar and continue beating until mixture will form soft peaks. Fold into pudding. Chill, if desired.
- Just before serving, stir in sherry. Serve over cake or fruit. Makes 6 servings.

CREAMY CHEESE BLINTZES

A delectable dessert treat, this Jewish version of crêpes

▌ *From 15 to 30 minutes to prepare*

2 eggs
1 package (4-serving) ★ Jell-O
  pudding — vanilla flavor
½ cup light cream, half and
  half or milk

1 package (8 oz.) cream cheese,
  softened*
1 egg yolk
1 tablespoon sugar
2 tablespoons butter or margarine

*Or use 1 cup sieved cottage cheese

- Beat eggs until light anf frothy with rotary beater, electric mixer or in electric blender. Beat in pudding mix and cream. For each crêpe, pour ¼ cup batter into hot well-buttered skillet. Turn to brown both sides.
- Combine cream cheese, egg yolk and sugar in bowl. Place about 1 tablespoon of cheese mixture on each crêpe. Roll up, tucking in ends. Sauté in butter in skillet, turning to brown both sides. Serve warm topped with sour cream or sprinkled with confectioners sugar, if desired. Makes six 7-inch crêpes or 3 servings.

VIENNESE MOCHA TORTE

Over 30 minutes to prepare

1 package (2-layer) chocolate
  or devil's food cake mix or
  pudding-included cake mix
1 package (4-serving) ☆ Jell-O
  instant pudding — chocolate
  or chocolate fudge flavor
4 eggs
1 cup water
½ cup oil

2 cups cold milk
1 envelope Dream Whip
  whipped topping mix
1 package (6-serving) ☆ Jell-O
  instant pudding — chocolate
  or chocolate fudge flavor
¼ cup cooled brewed Maxwell
  House coffee
1 jar (10 oz.) apricot preserves

• Combine cake mix, 4-serving size pudding mix, eggs, water and oil in large mixer
  bowl. Blend, then beat at medium speed of electric mixer for 4 minutes. Pour into
  two greased and floured 9-inch layer pans. Bake at 350° for 30 to 35 minutes,
  or until cake tester inserted in center comes out clean and cakes begin to pull
  away from sides of pans. *Do not underbake.* Cool in pans about 15 minutes.
  Remove from pans and finish cooling on racks. Split cakes, making 4 layers.
• Combine milk, whipped topping mix and 6-serving size pudding mix in deep
  narrow-bottom mixer bowl. Beat at low speed until well blended. Gradually increase
  speed to high and whip until mixture forms soft peaks, 4 to 6 minutes.
• Sprinkle each layer with 1 tablespoon of the coffee. Spread half of the jam on one
  layer and top with about 1 cup of the frosting. Add the second layer and spread
  with 1 cup of frosting. Repeat layers. Garnish with chocolate curls, if desired. Chill.

71

POPPY SEED CAKE

From Eastern Europe, a tube cake with a distinctive flavor

▨ Over 30 minutes to prepare

1 package (2-layer) yellow cake mix or pudding-included cake mix	4 eggs
	1 cup (½ pt.) sour cream
1 package (4-serving) ☆ Jell-O instant pudding— vanilla flavor*	¼ cup oil
	½ cup cream sherry
	¼ cup poppy seed

Or use ★ Jell-O pudding— vanilla flavor

• Combine all ingredients in large mixer bowl. Blend, then beat at medium speed of electric mixer for 4 minutes. Pour into greased and floured 10-inch tube or fluted tube pan. Bake at 350° for 50 minutes or until cake tester inserted in center comes out clean and cake begins to pull away from sides of pan. <u>Do not underbake.</u> Cool in pan 15 minutes. Remove from pan and finish cooling on rack.

FRENCH APPLE CAKE

Like tangy French apple pie? Here's the cake version

▨ Over 30 minutes to prepare

1 package (2-layer) yellow cake mix	⅓ cup sour cream
	½ cup chopped raisins
1 package (4-serving) ☆ Jell-O instant pudding— lemon flavor	1 cup chopped peeled tart apple
4 eggs	½ teaspoon cinnamon
½ cup water	¼ teaspoon nutmeg
⅓ cup oil	Tart lemon glaze

• Combine cake mix, pudding mix, eggs, water, oil and sour cream in large mixer bowl. Blend, then beat at medium speed of electric mixer for 4 minutes. Combine raisins, apple and spices. Mix well and stir into batter. Pour into greased and floured 10-inch fluted tube pan. Bake at 350° for 50 to 55 minutes or until cake tester inserted in center comes out clean and cake begins to pull away from sides of pan. <u>Do not underbake.</u> Cool in pan about 15 minutes. Remove from pan and finish cooling on rack. Top with Tart Lemon Glaze.

TART LEMON GLAZE: Place 1 tablespoon softened butter or margarine in small bowl. Gradually stir in 1 cup sifted confectioners sugar, blending well. Add 1 tablespoon lemon juice. Add 1 to 2 teaspoons milk or water, a teaspoon at a time, until mixture is of glaze consistency. Spread over top of cake and allow to run down sides. Makes about ½ cup or enough for a 10-inch tube or fluted tube cake or two 9x5-inch loaf cakes.

RUM BABA CAKE

Quick way with that French dessert cake— fruity, rich and easy

📱 *Over 30 minutes to prepare*

1 package (2-layer) yellow cake mix	1 can (12 oz.) apricot nectar
1 package (4-serving) ☆ Jell-O instant pudding— lemon flavor	¼ cup oil
4 eggs	¼ cup currants
	1 cup sugar
	½ cup rum

• Combine cake mix, pudding mix, eggs, 1 cup of the apricot nectar, oil and currants in large mixer bowl. Blend well, then beat at medium speed of electric mixer for 4 minutes. Pour into greased and floured 10-inch tube or fluted tube pan. Bake at 350° for 55 to 60 minutes or until cake tester inserted in center comes out clean and cake begins to pull away from sides of pan. <u>Do not underbake.</u> Cool in pan about 15 minutes.

• Meanwhile, combine remaining apricot nectar and sugar in saucepan. Bring to a boil and boil 5 minutes, stirring constantly. Stir in rum.

• Remove cake from pan onto serving plate and prick with cake tester or wooden pick. Slowly and carefully spoon rum syrup over warm cake. Serve cake wedges topped with whipped topping, if desired.

NAPOLEONS IN THE ROUND

Homemade French pastry made easy! Frozen patty shells, custard mix do it

📱 *Over 30 minutes to prepare*

1 package (10 oz.) frozen patty shells	1 cup thawed Cool Whip non-dairy whipped topping
1 package (3 oz.) Jell-O Americana golden egg custard mix	½ cup confectioners sugar
1¼ cups milk	2½ teaspoons milk
1 tablespoon sherry wine (optional)	1 square Baker's semi-sweet chocolate
	2 teaspoons butter or margarine

• Bake patty shells as directed on package. Remove soft pastry from centers, reserving crisp baked tops. Cool.

• Blend custard mix with milk in saucepan. Bring quickly to a boil, stirring constantly. (Mixture will be thin.) Add sherry. Chill until thickened, about 1 hour.

• Stir chilled custard mixture until smooth. Blend in whipped topping. Spoon into patty shells and replace tops. Combine confectioners sugar and milk. Spread over tops and outer rims of shells. Melt chocolate with butter over low heat and drizzle over icing. Chill at least 1 hour. Refrigerate any leftover pastries. Makes 6 servings.

ITALIAN RICOTTA PIE

Creamy and rich with cheese, and you can make it in minutes

📖 *Less than 15 minutes to prepare*

1 package (8 oz.) cream cheese,
   softened
1 cup milk
1 tablespoon sherry wine
1 cup ricotta cheese
1 package (4-serving) ☆ Jell-O
   instant pudding — lemon
   or vanilla flavor

⅓ cup chopped
   toasted almonds
2 tablespoons chopped
   mixed candied fruits
1 baked 9-inch
   graham cracker crumb
   crust or pie shell,
   cooled*

*Or use 8-inch springform pan with graham cracker crumb crust, cooled

• Beat cream cheese until very soft. Gradually blend in ½ cup of the milk, beating until smooth. Add remaining milk, the sherry, ricotta cheese and pudding mix. Beat for 1 minute or until well blended. Fold in almonds and fruits. Spoon into pie shell. Chill until firm, at least 2 hours. Garnish with additional chopped candied fruit, if desired.

SWISS MOCHA PIE

Rich and fluffy, with that Swiss blend of coffee and chocolate

🍴 *Less than 15 minutes to prepare*

1¾ cups cold milk
⅓ cup coffee liqueur*
1 envelope Dream Whip
    whipped topping mix

1 package (6-serving) ☆ Jell-O
    instant pudding — chocolate
    or chocolate fudge flavor
1 baked 9-inch pie shell, cooled

Or use ⅓ cup strong coffee

• Combine milk, liqueur, whipped topping mix and pudding mix in deep narrow-bottom bowl. Beat slowly with rotary beater or at lowest speed of electric mixer until well blended. Gradually increase beating speed and beat until mixture will form soft peaks, about 3 to 6 minutes. Spoon into pie shell. Chill about 3 hours, or freeze until firm.

FRENCH CHERRY PIE

A piquant mix of flavors in a quick-to-make homemade dessert

🍴 *Less than 15 minutes to prepare*

1 cup cold milk
1 cup (½ pt.) sour cream
¼ teaspoon almond extract
1 package (4-serving) ☆ Jell-O
    instant pudding — vanilla
    or French vanilla flavor

1 baked 8-inch pie shell,
    cooled
1 can (21 oz.) cherry
    pie filling

• Combine milk, sour cream and almond extract in bowl. Add pudding mix. Beat slowly with rotary beater or at lowest speed of electric mixer until well blended, about 1 minute. Pour immediately into pie shell. Chill 2 hours. Spoon cherry pie filling over each serving.

CARIBBEAN PINEAPPLE PIE

A coconut crust, a splash of rum...a memorable Island treat

🍴 *Less than 15 minutes to prepare*

1 package (4-serving) ☆ Jell-O
    instant pudding —
    vanilla flavor
3 to 4 tablespoons rum
1½ cups sour cream
1 tablespoon sugar

1 teaspoon lime juice
1 can (8¼ oz.) crushed
    pineapple in syrup,
    drained
1 baked 9-inch quick coconut
    crust, cooled (p. 29)

• Combine pudding mix, rum, sour cream, sugar and lime juice in bowl. Beat just until well blended, about 1 minute. Fold in drained pineapple. Spoon mixture into crust. Chill until set, at least 3 hours. Garnish with whipped topping and maraschino cherries, if desired.

MEXICAN CHOCOLATE PIE

Chocolate gets the spark of cinnamon, in the South of the Border way

🥛 *Less than 15 minutes to prepare*

2¼ cups cold milk
1 envelope Dream Whip
   whipped topping mix
1 package (6-serving) ☆ Jell-O
   instant pudding — chocolate
   or chocolate fudge flavor

½ teaspoon cinnamon
1 baked 9-inch pie shell
   or graham cracker
   crumb crust,
   cooled

• Combine milk, whipped topping mix, pudding mix and cinnamon in deep narrow-bottom bowl. Beat slowly until well blended. Gradually increase beating speed and beat until mixture will form soft peaks, about 3 to 6 minutes. Spoon into pie shell. Chill about 3 hours, or freeze until firm. Garnish with whipped topping and sprinkle with additional cinnamon, if desired.

MEDITERRANEAN PISTACHIO EASIER PIE

Easy version of the honey-and-shredded-wheat desserts of the Near East

🗋 *From 15 to 30 minutes to prepare*

1 cup finely crushed whole wheat wafers
2 tablespoons butter or margarine, melted
2 tablespoons honey
1 package (4-serving) ☆ Jell-O instant pudding — pistachio flavor

1 ¾ cups cold milk
1 cup thawed Cool Whip non-dairy whipped topping
1 tablespoon honey

• Mix wafer crumbs with butter and 2 tablespoons honey. Press firmly onto bottom and sides of 8-inch pie pan. Chill about 15 minutes.
• Combine pudding mix and milk in bowl. Beat slowly with rotary beater or at lowest speed of electric mixer for 1 minute. Pour into crumb-lined 8-inch pie pan. Chill 1 hour. Garnish chilled pie with dollops of whipped topping and drizzle with 1 tablespoon honey.

STRAWBERRY ROMANOFF PIE

Fit for a czar, creamy strawberry with a dash of orange

🗋 *Over 30 minutes to prepare*

1 package (4-serving) ★ Jell-O pudding — vanilla flavor
1 package (3 oz.) Jell-O brand gelatin — strawberry flavor
2 cups water
3 tablespoons orange liqueur*

1 container (4 ½ oz.) Cool Whip non-dairy whipped topping, thawed
1 pint strawberries, sliced
1 baked 9-inch pie shell, cooled

Or use 3 tablespoons orange juice

• Combine pudding mix, gelatin and water in saucepan. Cook and stir over medium heat until mixture comes to a boil. Add liqueur and chill until thickened. (To hasten chilling time, place bowl of pudding mixture in larger bowl of ice and water; stir until thickened.)
• Fold whipped topping into chilled mixture. Add strawberries, reserving a few for garnish, if desired. Pour into pie shell and chill about 2 hours. Garnish with additional whipped topping and reserved strawberries, if desired.

IRISH COFFEE PIE

Coffee laced with whisky, a creamy topping...all in an easy pie

🗋 *Less than 15 minutes to prepare*

2 ½ cups cold milk
2 tablespoons Irish whisky or blended whisky
1 package (6-serving) ☆ Jell-O instant pudding — vanilla flavor

2 teaspoons instant Maxwell House coffee
1 baked 9-inch pie shell, cooled

• Pour milk and whisky into deep narrow-bottom bowl. Add pudding mix and instant coffee. Beat slowly with rotary beater or at lowest speed of electric mixer for 1 minute. Pour at once into pie shell. Chill 3 hours. Garnish with whipped topping and sprinkle with cinnamon, if desired.

Fabulous Company Desserts

They look beautiful, and that's the first "must" in a company dessert. And, they taste delicious, and that's the second— and most important— requirement. And for all their great good looks and their great taste, all are a lot easier to make than they look, thanks to pudding. Pudding is the foundation you build your desserts— and your reputation— on.

There's a spectacular Baked Alaska that could well put you on a "best cook" pedestal; no one need know it's a snap to make. There's an elegant— and simple— Fruit-and-Pudding Compote that could be the highlight of a summer patio party. There's a heavenly Almond Fudge Pie that could easily become "your" pie, the one everyone wants the recipe for. The rich German Sweet Chocolate Cake that will probably become a tradition at every family gathering. And this Double Almond Torte: you make two at once, then give your guests a choice of two flavorful toppings.

Want to earn a reputation as a great hostess? Build your party around great desserts like these.

DOUBLE ALMOND TORTES

One cake turns into two company tortes, with a choice of flavors

📷 *Over 30 minutes to prepare*

1 package (2-layer) yellow
　cake mix
1 package (4-serving) ☆ Jell-O
　instant pudding—
　vanilla flavor
4 eggs
1 cup water
¼ cup oil

1 teaspoon almond extract
½ cup chopped toasted almonds
1 cup red raspberry or
　strawberry preserves
1 cup apricot or peach
　preserves
1 cup sliced almonds
Confectioners sugar

- Combine cake mix, pudding mix, eggs, water, oil and extract in large mixer bowl. Blend, then beat at medium speed of electric mixer for 4 minutes. Stir in chopped almonds. Pour into 2 greased and floured 9-inch layer pans. Bake at 350° for 30 to 35 minutes or until cake tester inserted in center comes out clean and cake begins to pull away from sides of pan. <u>Do not underbake</u>. Cool in pans 15 minutes. Remove from pans and finish cooling on racks.
- Split each layer horizontally, making 4 layers. On each bottom layer spread ⅔ cup of the preserves, raspberry on one, apricot on the other. Sprinkle each with ½ cup of sliced almonds. If desired, cut 3-inch circles from centers of top layers. Place over bottom layers. Spread each with ⅓ cup of preserves and sprinkle generously with confectioners sugar. Makes 2 tortes.

GLAZED MOCHA CAKE

Liqueurs added to the cake and glaze give a rich mocha flavor

🔲 *Over 30 minutes to prepare*

1 package (2-layer) chocolate
   cake mix
1 package (4-serving) ☆ Jell-O
   instant pudding—
   chocolate flavor
4 eggs
¾ cup strong brewed
   Maxwell House coffee

8 tablespoons coffee liqueur
8 tablespoons crème de cacao
   liqueur
¼ cup oil
2 tablespoons strong brewed
   Maxwell House coffee
1 cup sifted confectioners
   sugar

• Combine cake mix, pudding mix, eggs, ¾ cup coffee, 6 tablespoons each of the liqueurs and the oil in mixer bowl. Blend, then beat at medium speed of electric mixer for 4 minutes. Pour into greased and floured 10-inch tube or fluted tube pan. Bake at 350° for 45 to 50 minutes or until cake tester inserted in center comes out clean and cake begins to pull away from sides of pan. <u>Do not underbake.</u> Cool in pan 15 minutes.
• Make glaze by combining 2 tablespoons coffee, remaining liqueurs and the confectioners sugar. Blend well. Remove cake from pan onto rack and poke with cake tester or wooden pick. Gradually spoon glaze over warm cake until completely absorbed. Cool.

BOURBON PRUNE CAKE

Moist and special with its glossy bourbon glaze. Our tasters loved it!

🔲 *Over 30 minutes to prepare*

1 package (2-layer) yellow
   cake mix
1 package (4-serving) ☆ Jell-O
   instant pudding— butter
   pecan or vanilla flavor
4 eggs
¼ cup oil

1 package (12 oz.) pitted
   prunes, chopped
1 cup water
½ cup chopped nuts
   (optional)
1 teaspoon cinnamon
Bourbon glaze

• Combine cake mix, pudding mix, eggs, oil, prunes, water, nuts and cinnamon in large mixer bowl. Blend, then beat at medium speed of electric mixer for 4 minutes. Pour into greased and floured 10-inch tube pan. Bake at 325° for about 1 hour and 25 minutes or until cake tester inserted in center comes out clean and cake begins to pull away from sides of pan. <u>Do not underbake.</u> Cool in pan 15 minutes.
• Invert cake onto serving plate and prick with cake tester or wooden pick. Carefully spoon Bourbon Glaze over warm cake. Garnish with whipped topping, if desired.
BOURBON GLAZE: Combine 1 cup sugar, ½ cup butter or margarine and ¼ cup water in saucepan. Cook and stir until mixture comes to a boil. Boil 5 minutes, stirring constantly. Remove from heat. Stir in ¼ cup bourbon.

BACARDI RUM CAKE

A winner everywhere, with its nutty topping, mellow flavor

🥫 *Over 30 minutes to prepare*

1 cup chopped pecans or walnuts
1 package (2-layer) yellow cake mix
1 package (4-serving) ☆ Jell-O
    instant pudding — vanilla flavor
4 eggs
½ cup water
¼ cup oil

½ cup Bacardi® dark rum
    (80 proof)
1 cup sugar
½ cup butter or margarine
¼ cup water
½ cup Bacardi® dark rum
    (80 proof)

- Sprinkle nuts evenly in bottom of greased and floured 10-inch tube or fluted tube pan.
- Combine cake mix, pudding mix, eggs, ½ cup water, oil and ½ cup rum in large mixer bowl. Blend, then beat at medium speed of electric mixer for 4 minutes. Pour into pan. Bake at 325° for about 1 hour or until cake tester inserted in center comes out clean and cake begins to pull away from sides of pan. <u>Do not underbake.</u> Cool in pan 15 minutes.
- Meanwhile, make syrup by combining sugar, butter and ¼ cup water in saucepan. Cook and stir until mixture comes to a boil. Boil 5 minutes, stirring constantly. Stir in ½ cup rum and bring just to a boil. Invert cake onto serving plate and prick with cake tester or wooden pick. Carefully spoon warm syrup over warm cake.

Bacardi is a registered trademark of Bacardi & Company Limited

GERMAN SWEET CHOCOLATE CAKE

A special-occasion cake layered with nutty coconut filling

🔲 *Over 30 minutes to prepare*

1 package (2-layer) yellow
   cake mix
1 package (4-serving) ☆ Jell-O
   instant pudding— vanilla flavor
1 package (4 oz.)
   Baker's German's
   sweet chocolate, melted

4 eggs
1¼ cups buttermilk
   or milk
¼ cup oil
   Easy coconut-pecan
   filling

• Combine cake mix, pudding mix, chocolate, eggs, buttermilk and oil in large mixer bowl. Blend, then beat at medium speed of electric mixer for 4 minutes. Pour into 3 greased and floured 8-or 9-inch layer pans. Bake at 350° for 30 minutes or until cake tester inserted in center comes out clean and cake begins to pull away from sides of pans. <u>Do not underbake</u>. Cool in pans about 15 minutes. Remove from pans and finish cooling on racks. Fill and frost with Coconut-Pecan Filling.

EASY COCONUT-PECAN FILLING: Combine ¾ cup light corn syrup and 1 package (6-serving) ☆ Jell-O instant pudding— butter pecan or vanilla flavor— in bowl, blending well. Gradually stir in 1 cup evaporated milk. Add about 2 cups Baker's Angel Flake coconut and ½ cup chopped pecans. Chill 10 minutes. Makes 2½ cups or enough to fill and top three 8- or 9-inch layers.

CHOCOLATE-COCONUT CAKE

Inside this luscious chocolate tube cake is a nice surprise— a crunchy coconut layer

🔲 *Over 30 minutes to prepare*

2 egg whites
   Dash of salt
⅓ cup sugar
2 tablespoons
   all-purpose flour
1¾ cups (about) Baker's
   Angel Flake or
   cookie coconut

1 package (2-layer) chocolate cake
   mix or pudding-included cake mix
1 package (4-serving) ☆ Jell-O
   instant pudding— chocolate flavor
2 eggs
2 egg yolks
1¼ cups water
⅓ cup oil

• Beat egg whites with salt until foamy throughout. Gradually add ⅓ cup sugar and continue beating until mixture will form stiff shiny peaks. Blend in flour and coconut. Set aside.
• Combine remaining ingredients in large mixer bowl. Blend, then beat at medium speed of electric mixer for 4 minutes. Pour one-third of batter into greased and floured 10-inch fluted tube pan. Spoon in coconut mixture and top with remaining batter. Bake at 350° for 50 to 55 minutes or until cake tester inserted in center comes out clean and cake begins to pull away from sides of pan. <u>Do not underbake</u>. Cool in pan 15 minutes. Remove from pan and finish cooling on rack.

PARTY NAPOLEON

Saltine crackers are the easy "pastry" secret to this delicious giant Napoleon

📦 From 15 to 30 minutes to prepare

32 square saltine crackers
¼ cup butter or margarine, melted
1 package (4-serving) ☆ Jell-O
instant pudding — vanilla flavor

1 envelope Dream Whip
whipped topping mix
1¼ cups cold milk
Confectioners sugar

• Break crackers into small pieces in bowl. Add butter and toss lightly. Place in shallow pan and bake at 350° for about 10 minutes stirring 2 or 3 times, until golden brown. Cool.

• Line bottom and sides of 8x4-inch loaf pan with wax paper, letting paper extend 2 inches over sides.

• Combine pudding mix, whipped topping mix and milk in deep narrow-bottom bowl. Beat slowly with electric mixer until well blended. Gradually increase beating speed and beat until mixture will form soft peaks, 4 to 6 minutes. Arrange one-fourth of the toasted cracker pieces in bottom of lined loaf pan. Top with 1¼ cups pudding mixture. Repeat layers twice. Arrange remaining crackers over top. Chill 4 to 5 hours. Lift loaf from pan and remove paper. Sprinkle top with confectioners sugar. Makes 6 servings.

QUICK CHOCOLATE LOAF

Make it in just minutes, then chill and freeze and it's ready for guests

📦 Less than 15 minutes to prepare

1½ cups cold milk
1 envelope
Dream Whip
whipped topping mix

1 package (4-serving) ☆ Jell-O
instant pudding — chocolate
or chocolate fudge flavor
12 ladyfingers, split*

° Or use an 8-ounce pound cake, thinly sliced and cut into strips

• Combine milk, whipped topping mix and pudding mix in deep narrow-bottom bowl. Beat slowly until well blended. Gradually increase beating speed and beat until mixture will form soft peaks, about 4 to 6 minutes.

• Line an 8x4-inch loaf pan or 1½-quart loaf dish with wax paper. Line bottom and sides with split ladyfingers. Spoon in pudding mixture. Chill or freeze until firm. Invert onto serving platter, remove wax paper and cut in slices. Makes 6 servings.

CHOCOLATE WAFER LOG

Just chocolate wafers and a quick-to-make pudding filling...and delectable

From 15 to 30 minutes to prepare

1 cup cold milk
1 package (4-serving) ☆ Jell-O
   instant pudding — any flavor
1 container (4 ½ oz.) Cool Whip
   non-dairy whipped
   topping, thawed

1 package (about 38) thin
   chocolate wafers
Grated chocolate or crushed
   peppermint candy

- Combine milk and pudding mix in bowl. Beat slowly with rotary beater or at lowest speed of electric mixer until well blended, 1 or 2 minutes. Let stand 5 minutes. Blend in 1 cup whipped topping.
- Spread cookies with filling and stack in groups of 6 or 8. Place stacks carefully on square of wax paper to form one long roll. Wrap in the paper and chill 2 to 3 hours.
- Just before serving, remove wax paper and place roll on serving plate. Spread remaining whipped topping over entire roll. Sprinkle with grated chocolate. Cut diagonally into slices. Store any leftover cake in refrigerator. Makes 6 to 8 servings.

BAVARIAN CREAM

A classic...light and fluffy, but amazingly rich

Over 30 minutes to prepare

1 package (4-serving) ★ Jell-O
   pudding — chocolate, milk
   chocolate or vanilla flavor
¼ cup sugar
1 envelope unflavored gelatin
Dash of salt

1 egg, slightly beaten
2 cups milk
1 teaspoon vanilla
¼ cup ground nuts (optional)
1 envelope Dream Whip
   whipped topping mix

- Combine pudding mix, sugar, gelatin and salt in saucepan. Blend egg with milk and add to pudding mixture, blending well. Cook and stir over medium heat until mixture comes to a *full* boil. Remove from heat and add vanilla. Cover surface with plastic wrap and chill at least 2 hours.
- Generously butter 4-cup mold and sprinkle with ground nuts. Prepare whipped topping mix as directed on package. Beat chilled pudding until creamy and blend in prepared whipped topping. Spoon into mold. Chill until firm, at least 2 hours. Unmold and garnish with additional prepared whipped topping, if desired. Makes 8 servings.

BAKED ALASKA

A party classic you can make ahead and freeze

🔲 *Over 30 minutes to prepare*

1 package (6-serving) ★ Jell-O	**3 cups thawed Cool Whip**
pudding — any flavor	**non-dairy whipped topping**
¼ cup sugar	**6 egg whites**
3 cups milk	**¾ cup sugar**

- Combine pudding mix, ¼ cup sugar and milk in saucepan. Cook and stir over medium heat until mixture comes to a <u>full</u> boil. Remove from heat. Cover surface with plastic wrap and chill.
- Beat chilled pudding until creamy. Blend in whipped topping. Pour into 1½-quart metal bowl and freeze for 1 hour. Beat with rotary beater or electric mixer until smooth but not completely melted. Freeze until firm, about 4 hours or overnight.
- Beat egg whites until foamy throughout. Gradually beat in ¾ cup sugar and continue beating until mixture will form stiff shiny peaks.
- Unmold frozen pudding mixture and place on wooden board which has been covered with brown paper or aluminum foil. Cover pudding completely with meringue. Bake at 500° for 2 to 5 minutes or until meringue is lightly browned. Immediately slip dessert off board onto serving platter and serve, or store in freezer until ready to serve. Makes 10 to 12 servings.

FLUFFY CHOCOLATE SOUFFLÉ

Soufflé shy? Now pudding takes out the work and the risk!

🍮 *Over 30 minutes to prepare*

1 package (4-serving) ★ Jell-O
   pudding— chocolate or
   chocolate fudge flavor
Dash of salt

3 egg yolks, well beaten
1¼ cups milk
1 teaspoon vanilla
3 egg whites

- Combine pudding mix, salt, egg yolks and milk in saucepan. Cook and stir over medium heat until mixture comes to a <u>full</u> boil. Remove from heat. Stir vigorously until smooth. Cool about 5 minutes, stirring once or twice. Add vanilla.
- Beat egg whites until soft peaks form. Fold in pudding mixture gently but thoroughly. Pour into greased 1-quart soufflé or baking dish. Place dish in pan of hot water and bake at 350° about 1 hour. Serve hot or cold, with light cream or custard sauce, if desired. (Warm soufflé will be light and fluffy; chilled soufflé settles as it cools and has a fudgy texture.) Makes 8 servings.

FRUIT-AND-PUDDING COMPOTE

Luscious fresh fruit layered with liqueur-sparked pudding...beautiful to serve

🍮 *From 15 to 30 minutes to prepare*

1 ¾ cups cold milk
1 tablespoon orange liqueur
   or orange juice
1 package (4-serving) ☆ Jell-O
   instant pudding—
   vanilla flavor

1 container (4½ oz.) Cool Whip
   non-dairy whipped topping,
   thawed
6 cups fresh fruits (blueberries,
   melon balls, raspberries,
   sliced strawberries,
   bananas, peaches)

- Combine milk, liqueur and pudding mix in bowl. Beat slowly with rotary beater or at lowest speed of electric mixer for 1 minute. Add 1 cup of the whipped topping and beat 1 minute longer, just until blended. Arrange half the fruit in large serving bowl. Add pudding mixture and top with remaining fruit. Garnish with remaining whipped topping. Makes 16 servings.

BOSTON CREAM PARFAIT

Those favorite Boston Cream Pie flavors now in an easy parfait version

🍮 *Less than 15 minutes to prepare*

1 package (4-serving) ☆ Jell-O
   instant pudding—
   vanilla flavor*
2 cups cold milk

2 tablespoons chocolate syrup
1 cup thawed Cool Whip
   non-dairy whipped topping

*Or use ★ Jell-O pudding— vanilla flavor

- Prepare pudding mix with milk as directed on package for pudding. (If using cooked pudding, chill.) Pour half the pudding into 6 parfait glasses. Top with chocolate syrup, whipped topping and remaining pudding mixture. Chill. Garnish with additional whipped topping and chocolate syrup, if desired. Makes 6 servings.

ALMOND FUDGE PIE

One of the richest, most chocolatey pies you've tasted!

▯ *From 15 to 30 minutes to prepare*

1 package (6-serving) ★ Jell-O
   pudding— chocolate
   fudge flavor
3 tablespoons brown sugar
2½ cups milk
2 eggs, slightly beaten

2 tablespoons butter or
   margarine
¼ teaspoon almond extract
½ cup chopped toasted almonds
1 baked 9-inch pie shell,
   cooled

Combine pudding mix, sugar and ½ cup of the milk in saucepan. Blend in eggs, then stir in remaining milk. Cook and stir over medium heat until mixture comes to a full boil. Remove from heat. Blend in butter and extract. Stir in almonds. Cool 5 minutes, stirring twice. Pour into pie shell. Cover surface with plastic wrap. Chill 3 hours. Garnish with whipped topping and toasted slivered almonds, if desired.

DAIQUIRI PIE

That refreshing tropical treat transformed into a cool and luscious pie

▯ *Over 30 minutes to prepare*

1 package (4-serving) ★ Jell-O
   pudding— lemon flavor
1 package (3 oz.) Jell-O
   brand gelatin—
   lime flavor
⅓ cup sugar
2½ cups water

2 eggs, slightly beaten
½ cup light rum
1 container (4½ oz.) Cool Whip
   non-dairy whipped
   topping, thawed
1 baked 9-inch graham cracker
   crumb crust, cooled

Combine pudding mix, gelatin and sugar in saucepan. Stir in ½ cup of the water and eggs. Blend well. Add remaining water and cook and stir over medium heat until mixture comes to a full boil. Remove from heat. Stir in rum. Chill. (To hasten chilling, place bowl of pudding mixture in larger bowl of ice and water. Stir until cold, about 10 to 15 minutes.)

Blend whipped topping into chilled pudding mixture. Spoon into pie crust and chill until firm, about 2 hours.

BRANDY ALEXANDER PIE

Highlight of any party, this elegant cordial pie

▯ *Less than 15 minutes to prepare*

2 cups cold milk
2 tablespoons brandy
2 tablespoons crème de cacao liqueur
1 envelope Dream Whip
   whipped topping mix

1 package (6-serving) ☆ Jell-O
   instant pudding—
   vanilla flavor
1 baked 9-inch pie shell,
   cooled

Combine milk, brandy, liqueur, whipped topping mix and pudding mix in deep narrow-bottom mixer bowl. Beat at low speed of electric mixer until well blended. Gradually increase beating speed and beat until mixture will form soft peaks, about 3 to 6 minutes. Spoon into pie shell. Chill about 3 hours or freeze until firm. Garnish with prepared whipped topping and chocolate curls, if desired.

PRALINE ICE CREAM PIE

Rich, creamy and crunchy...a delicious homemade pie

🗋 *Over 30 minutes to prepare*

2 tablespoons light brown
   sugar
2 tablespoons butter or
   margarine
⅓ cup chopped nuts
1 lightly baked 9-inch pie shell

1½ cups cold milk
1 cup (½ pt.) vanilla ice
   cream, softened
1 package (6-serving) ☆ Jell-O
   instant pudding —
   butter pecan flavor

- Combine brown sugar, butter and nuts in saucepan. Heat until butter is melted. Pour into pie shell and bake at 450° for 5 minutes. Cool.
- Thoroughly blend milk and ice cream in bowl. Add pudding mix. Beat slowly with rotary beater or at lowest speed of electric mixer until blended, about 1 minute. Pour immediately into pie shell. Chill until set, about 3 hours. Garnish with whipped topping and additional chopped nuts, if desired.

TRIPLE LAYER PIE

A layer of chocolate, then vanilla, then chocolate-sparked topping

🔲 *From 15 to 30 minutes to prepare*

1 package (4-serving) ☆ Jell-O
   instant pudding—chocolate flavor*
1¾ cups cold milk
1 baked 9-inch pie shell, cooled
1 package (4-serving) ☆ Jell-O
   instant pudding—vanilla or
   coconut cream flavor*

1¾ cups milk
1 tablespoon chocolate
   syrup or cocoa
1 cup thawed Cool Whip
   non-dairy whipped
   topping

*Or use ★ Jell-O pudding—chocolate or chocolate fudge
and vanilla or coconut cream flavors*

- Prepare chocolate pudding mix as directed on package for pie, reducing milk to 1¾ cups. Pour into pie shell.
- Prepare vanilla pudding mix as directed on package for pie, reducing milk to 1¾ cups. Carefully pour over chocolate layer. (If using cooked pudding, chill about 3 hours.)
- Fold syrup into whipped topping. Spread over vanilla layer. Chill 3 hours.

CHOCOLATE CRUNCH PIE

Sweet chocolate flavors the pudding filling; nuts and coconut make a crunchy crust

🔲 *From 15 to 30 minutes to prepare*

⅓ cup butter or margarine
⅓ cup firmly packed brown sugar
⅓ cup chopped pecans
⅓ cup Baker's Angel Flake
   coconut
1 lightly baked 9-inch pie shell
1 package (6-serving) ★ Jell-O
   pudding—vanilla flavor

1 package (4 oz.) Baker's
   German's sweet chocolate,
   broken in pieces
2½ cups milk
1 cup thawed Cool Whip
   non-dairy whipped topping
   or prepared Dream Whip
   whipped topping

- Combine butter, brown sugar, pecans and coconut in saucepan. Heat until butter and sugar are melted. Spread in bottom of pie shell. Bake at 450° for 5 minutes or until bubbly. Cool.
- Combine pudding mix, chocolate and milk in saucepan. Cook and stir over medium heat until mixture comes to a _full bubbling boil_. Remove from heat and beat with wire whip or rotary beater to blend, if necessary. Cool 5 minutes, stirring occasionally. Pour into pie shell. Cover surface with plastic wrap. Chill at least 4 hours. Remove plastic wrap and garnish with whipped topping and additional coconut, if desired.

STRAWBERRY-CHEESE EASIER PIE

*Easy and elegant...cracker crust, piquant cheese layer,
strawberries and a pudding top*

🗂 *Over 30 minutes to prepare*

**1¼ cups crushed round buttery
crackers**
¼ cup butter or margarine, melted
**1 package (8 oz.) cream
cheese, softened**
2 tablespoons sugar
2 tablespoons milk
1 cup halved strawberries

**1 package (4-serving) ☆ Jell-O
instant pudding —
vanilla or lemon flavor**
1½ cups cold milk
**1 container (4½ oz.)
Cool Whip non-dairy
whipped topping,
thawed**

- *Combine crackers and butter and press into bottom of 8-inch square pan. Bake at 375° for 8 minutes. Cool.*
- *Beat cream cheese with sugar and 2 tablespoons milk in bowl until smooth. Spread evenly in crumb-lined pan. Arrange strawberries on cream cheese mixture.*
- *Combine pudding mix and 1½ cups milk in bowl. Beat slowly with rotary beater or at lowest speed of electric mixer until well blended, about 2 minutes. Fold in 1 cup of the whipped topping. Spoon over strawberries and chill until set, about 2 hours. Garnish with remaining whipped topping and additional strawberries, if desired. Cut into squares. Makes 9 servings.*

LEMON-GRAHAM EASIER PIE

■ *Over 30 minutes to prepare*

1 cup graham cracker crumbs
3 tablespoons sugar
¼ cup softened butter or margarine
1 envelope Dream Whip
   whipped topping mix

2½ cups cold milk
¼ cup lemon juice
1 teaspoon grated lemon rind
1 package (6-serving) ☆ Jell-O
   instant pudding—lemon flavor

Combine crumbs and sugar. Mix in butter. Press crumb mixture firmly on bottom of 9-inch square pan, reserving two tablespoons for garnish, if desired. Bake at 375° for 8 minutes. Cool thoroughly.
Meanwhile, prepare whipped topping mix as directed on package. Set aside. Combine milk, lemon juice, lemon rind and pudding mix in bowl. Beat slowly with rotary beater or at lowest speed of electric mixer until well blended, about 2 minutes. Blend into prepared whipped topping. Pour immediately into crumb-lined pan. Sprinkle with reserved crumbs. Freeze until firm, at least 4 hours. Remove pan from freezer about 30 minutes before serving. Makes 8 or 9 servings.

ORANGE-CHOCOLATE EASIER PIE

Here chocolate wafers make the crust...so simple!

■ *Less than 15 minutes to prepare*

18 chocolate wafers
1 package (4-serving) ☆ Jell-O
   instant pudding—vanilla flavor
1 cup milk
1 cup thawed Cool Whip non-
   dairy whipped topping

2 medium oranges, peeled
   and thinly sliced
3 tablespoons apricot
   preserves or orange
   marmalade
1 teaspoon water

Arrange half the cookies in bottom of 8-inch square pan. Combine pudding mix with milk in bowl. Beat slowly with rotary beater or at lowest speed of electric mixer until well blended, about 2 minutes. Fold in whipped topping. Pour half the pudding mixture over cookies in pan. Layer remaining cookies and remaining pudding mixture. Top with orange slices. Thin apricot preserves with water and spoon over oranges. Chill about 2 hours. Cut into squares. Makes 9 servings.

PINEAPPLE-CHEESE EASIER PIE

■ *From 15 to 30 minutes to prepare*

¾ cup graham cracker crumbs
2 tablespoons sugar
⅓ cup chopped toasted walnuts
3 tablespoons butter or
   margarine, melted
1 cup milk
1 cup canned pineapple juice

1 package (4-serving) ★ Jell-O
   pudding—vanilla, coconut
   cream or banana cream flavor
¼ cup sugar
1 package (8 oz.) cream cheese,
   cut into cubes

Combine graham cracker crumbs, 2 tablespoons sugar, nuts and butter. Press two-thirds of mixture into 8-inch square pan. Combine milk, pineapple juice, pudding mix, ¼ cup sugar and cream cheese in saucepan. Cook and stir over medium heat until mixture comes to a <u>full</u> boil. Remove from heat and beat with rotary beater until smooth. Pour into crumb-lined pan. Sprinkle with remaining crumb mixture. Chill until firm. Cut into squares. Makes 9 servings.

Index

★ *Jell-O pudding and pie filling*
☆ *Jell-O instant pudding and pie filling*
▣ *Jell-O Americana rice pudding, tapioca pudding or golden egg custard*

Designed by General Foods Corporate Design Center